# HOW THE RUSSIANS INVENTED BASEBALL

# HOW THE RUSSIANS INVENTED BASEBALL

## And Other Essays of Enlightenment

### JOHN LEO

Delacorte
Press

Published by
Delacorte Press
Bantam Doubleday Dell Publishing Group, Inc.
666 Fifth Avenue
New York, New York 10103

Acknowledgment is made to the following magazines and publishers in whose pages these articles first appeared:
*Bird Watcher's Digest:* "The Luckiest Bird-Watcher in America."
*Child* magazine: "Some Assembly Required."
*Decorating Remodeling:* "Manly about the House."
East Hampton *Star:* "Have a Martini—the Birds Will Be Right Along."
*The New York Times:* "Keep Irish Meusel out of Cooperstown."
*Time:* "We Don't Say *Orgy* Anymore"; "Journalese, or Why English Is the Second Language of the Fourth Estate"; "Manila Envelopes *vs.* Kiev Chickens"; "Womenspeak *vs.* Mentalk"; "Why Men Don't Do Chores"; "Save Your Marriage, Just $19.95"; "Legal Valentines"; "Boy George and Blue Doorknob Pride Day"; "Firebelles in the Night"; "Beasts of the City"; "The Stewardi Have Stopped Smiling"; "Why All Villains Are Thin, Middle-Aged WASPS"; "Ophelia the Carnophobe"; "The Babe Ruth of Sex"; "The Return of the Sexual Squares"; "Searching High and Low for the Big O"; "How the Russians Invented Baseball."
*Vanity Fair:* "Sally Field Is Indomitable Yet Again."

*Book design by Richard Oriolo*

The trademark Delacorte Press ® is registered in the U.S. Patent and Trademark Office.
Library of Congress Cataloging in Publication Data
Leo, John.
How the Russians invented baseball and other essays of enlightenment.
1. Popular culture—Humor. I. Title
PN6162.L375   1989      814'.54   88-33596
ISBN 0-385-29758-0

Manufactured in the United States of America
Published simultaneously in Canada

August 1989

10  9  8  7  6  5  4  3  2  1

BG

# ACKNOWLEDGMENTS

About half of this material appeared in *Time* magazine, some of it in different form. Individual pieces are reprinted from *Vanity Fair, The New York Times, Child* magazine, the East Hampton *Star, Decorating Remodeling,* and *Bird Watcher's Digest.*

Thanks to E. Graydon Carter, Ray Cave, Roger Rosenblatt, and my editor, Jane Rosenman, for support and encouragement.

*For Jackie*

# Contents

Acknowledgments

WORDS WORDS WORDS

We Don't Say *Orgy* Anymore                                    3

Journalese, or Why English Is the Second
Language of the Fourth Estate                                  9

Manila Envelopes *vs.* Kiev Chickens                         24

Womenspeak *vs.* Mentalk                                     32

"We're the Folks at Unitox"                                  37


FUMBLING AROUND THE HOUSE

Why Men Don't Do Chores                                      45

Some Assembly Required                                       50

Save Your Marriage, Just $19.95                             56

Manly about the House                                       61

Legal Valentines                                            65


BOYS WILL BE BOYS

John Scanlon Meets St. Philomena                            73

Boy George and Blue Doorknob Pride Day                      80

Exclusive: Ronald Reagan's Memoirs!                         85

Stop the Press—Men Have Feelings Too                        89

Firebelles in the Night                                     93

Beasts of the City ....................................... 98

TOUCHY, TOUCHY

The Stewardi Aren't Smiling Anymore ............... 105
Why All Villains Are Thin,
Middle-Aged WASPS .................................... 110
Ophelia the Carnophobe ............................... 117
Sally Field Is Indomitable Yet Again ................ 122
Ralph and Wanda Fight Fair ........................... 127

SEX IN THE EIGHTIES: A SHORT HISTORY

The Babe Ruth of Sex ................................. 133
The Return of the Sexual Squares .................... 138
Searching High and Low for the Big O ............... 143
No F-Words, Please ................................... 148

BASEBALL, BIRDING, AND BLOWHARDS

How the Russians Invented Baseball .................. 155
Keep Irish Meusel Out of Cooperstown ............... 160
Spanky Predicts a Pennant Race ...................... 166
The Luckiest Bird-Watcher in America ................ 171
Have a Martini—the Birds
Will Be Right Along ................................... 175

# HOW THE RUSSIANS INVENTED BASEBALL

# WORDS
# WORDS
# WORDS

# We Don't Say *Orgy* Anymore

**R**alph and Wanda, the happily quarreling couple who bob up now and then in this book, were born one day during a pop-psych crisis in my back-of-the-book department at Time *magazine. As the writer of the Behavior section (sometimes it was called The Sexes), I was supposed to do a one-pager on a group of unusually moronic books on how to be a successful middle-aged person.*

*Rather than do it straight-faced, I created an argument between Wanda, a liberal feminist who loved each week's new therapy, and Ralph, a curmudgeonly masculinist who thought it was all nonsense. This early-phase Ralph & Wanda was a hit with readers, but not with my teenaged daughters, who remained moderately sullen for several weeks until I bit the bullet and inquired about what might be wrong. I was told firmly that Ralph got all*

*the good lines and Wanda insulted women by being entirely too*
*stupid to keep up with a mildly crazed hubby whom she never*
*should have married in the first place.*

*As an attentive father, I immediately gave Wanda fifty or*
*sixty extra IQ points. This had a large drawback—she was now*
*entirely too smart to serve as a simple foil, or to go around buying*
*books on how to transplant your psyche in thirty minutes through*
*Transylvanian meditation. But it was fairer. Ralph took some*
*heavy shots from his suddenly bright mate, though not as many as*
*my daughters would have liked. The heaviest mail came when*
*Wanda exploded over the refusal of Ralph, and virtually all mar-*
*ried males, to do more than one or two annual chores around the*
*house. My daughters, and (unaccountably) my wife, liked that one*
*too. In the following dialogue, the mismatched couple quarrel over*
*sexual euphemisms.*

**Wanda:** I got in late, Ralph. What happened today on *Search*
*for Yesterday?*

**Ralph:** The usual, my sweet. Craig is still sowing his wild oats.
Fenwick is wife-swapping with Brent. Cybele attended her first
orgy, where she fornicated with Brad, the recently rehabilitated
pervert.

**Wanda:** (Sigh.) You really must do something about your language.

**Ralph:** What's the matter? Too dirty?

**Wanda:** Too old. We don't use those kinds of words anymore.
To begin with, *wife-swapping* is sexist. It implies that women are

property. It was changed years ago to *mate-swapping*, then to *swinging*. Now two sex writers suggest we call it "expanding the circle of love." That may be a bit much. . . .

**Ralph:** Not at all, dearest. Circle expansion is fine with me. Where else did I go wrong?

**Wanda:** *Fornication.* To anyone born after 1900 and not directly employed by the Ayatollah Khomeini, it is known as premarital or nonmarital sex, and adultery is extramarital sex, comarital sex, or just extra sex. *Orgy* is now simply group sex. Since you spent a year reading *The Joy of Sex* and *More Joy,* you may remember that Alex Comfort suggests we call orgies "sharing."

**Ralph:** I love that word, Wanda. It brings out the total selflessness of an evening spent slaving over the needs of other people. Give me more of your sexual euphemisms. What do we call perverts these days?

**Wanda:** The last pervert died in 1957, Ralph. Nowadays we have sexual minorities and sexual variations, some of them involving sexual aids and sexual toys, and all of them indulged in by folks with alternate sexual preferences. *Perversion* is a nasty, judgmental word that is likely to hurt the feelings of variants everywhere. In *The Family Book about Sexuality*, Mary Calderone and Eric Johnson define perversion as "a term loosely applied to sexual behavior that the user of the term does not approve of."

**Ralph:** I couldn't have said it better, Wanda. Since there are no more perverts, I assume parents no longer have to worry about child molesters, but do you think that they could keep a nonjudgmental eye out for pedophilic variants?

**Wanda:** Don't be smart, Ralph. And I want you to avoid the term *promiscuous*. That's a male word for women who do what men have always done.

**Ralph:** What's the modern term?

**Wanda:** *Sexual variety* or *casual sex.* Helen Gurley Brown suggests that a woman who sleeps with two or more men in one week can simply be called "multifriended."

**Ralph:** You can never have too many friends, Wanda. Okay. I'm beginning to get the hang of this. Any affair is now a relationship. In the fifties we lusted after loose girls and pushovers, but in the eighties men search for their sexual identities with liberated women. Tots who play doctor are engaged in sexual rehearsal play. My dirty books are pornography, but yours are erotica. A woman who has never had an orgasm is not frigid or even nonorgasmic, but preorgasmic. Bluebeard, Catherine the Great, and Errol Flynn were multifriended, but I am married and single-friended with a woefully constricted circle of love. How am I doing so far?

**Wanda:** It's you, Ralph. Totally offensive.

**Ralph:** Let's plod on, my love. What's modernspeak for *masturbation*? Sexual self-enhancement?

**Wanda:** Self-pleasuring, sex for one, the first step in the process of sexualization, self-remedy for orgasmic dysfunction.

**Ralph:** And you don't even have to dress for it! What about *foreplay?*

**Wanda:** Out. It implies that what you males do is the main event. *Foreplay* is now genital pleasuring, sexual expressiveness, or a high stage of sensate-focus exercise.

**Ralph:** I suppose all this is done with a significant other in a primary meaningful relationship.

**Wanda:** Not necessarily, stodgy one. It can be in a satellite relationship, or with a partner you have just met and may not see again.

**Ralph:** You mean a one-night stand.

**Wanda:** A shabby, reactionary term. Call it a brief encounter. Helen Gurley Brown suggests we label it an instant liaison or a one-night friendship.

**Ralph:** Not good enough, my pet. Helen is trying hard. But for true obfuscation, all euphemisms should be poured into Latinate verbiage. How about a uninocturnal relationship? Or if it's a noonie, call it a self-limiting quotidian encounter.

**Wanda:** Ralph, I'm experiencing oral desire-phase dysfunction.

**Ralph:** What's that?

**Wanda:** I don't want to talk about it anymore.

**Ralph:** But we must, beloved. We must cleanse the mother tongue of preliberation pettifoggery. I assume that *mistress, kept* *woman, bimbo,* and *paramour* are somehow offensive, but what about the term *prostitute*?

**Wanda:** There's no good word yet. Those in the business don't seem to like it very much, so we tried *working girl,* which changed quickly to *working woman,* but that's the name of a magazine that appeals to female executives.

**Ralph:** Hmmm. I guess *ladies of the evening* won't do. How about *strolling sexual facilitators?* Or *free-lance orgasmetricians?*

**Wanda:** You are a difficult man, Ralph.

**Ralph:** And one ever eager to learn, light of my life. Now let me recast today's soapy occurrences on *Search for Yesterday.* Our friend Craig is expressing his sexual needs in a heartfelt but brief interpersonal exchange with a woman whose name he didn't catch. Fenwick and Brent are having extra sex in multilateral interfamilial relationships with each other's spouses. Cybele attended a sharing, where, amid an enormous pile of bodies, she encountered one belonging to Brad, the well-known variant, thus decisively augmenting her sexual growth. I believe I'll sign off, Wanda.

**Wanda:** Ralph, you'll pay for this.

# Journalese, or Why English Is the Second Language of the Fourth Estate

**A**s a cub reporter, columnist Richard Cohen of *The Washington Post* trudged out one day to interview a lawyer who had been described in many newspaper reports as "ruddy-faced." The man was woozily abusive and lurched about with such abandon that young Cohen instantly realized that the real meaning of *ruddy-faced* is drunk. This was his introduction to journalese, the fascinating second tongue acquired by most reporters as effortlessly as an Iranian toddler learns Farsi or a Marin County child learns psychobabble.

Fluency in journalese means learning all about "the right stuff," "life in the fast lane," and the vexing dilemma of being caught "between a rock and a hard place," the current Scylla-Charybdis image. The Middle East is "war-torn" or "strife-torn," except during those inexplicable moments when peace briefly breaks out. Then it is simply "much-troubled." Kuwait is located just east of the adjective *oil-rich,* and the Irish Republican Army lurks right behind the word *outlawed.*

Much of the difficulty of mastering journalese stems from its slight overlap with English. *Imposing,* for instance, when used to describe a male, retains its customary English meaning, but when used in reference to a female, it means "battle-axe." In journalese the word *chilling* has the very solemn task of modifying *scenario* (in nuclear weapons stories), *reminder* (in crime stories) and *effect* (any story on AIDS or the imminent repeal of the First Amendment), whereas in English it is merely something one does with white wine.

Some English words mean exactly the opposite in journalese. *Multitalented,* for example, means untalented, and is used to identify applause-starved entertainers who prance about with amazing pep and perspiration, but do nothing particularly well. *Community* means noncommunity, as in the intelligence community, the gay community, or the journalese-speaking community. Under this usage, everyone shooting everyone else in and around Beirut, say, could be fairly described as the Lebanese community.

*Feisty* refers to a person whom the journalist deems too short and too easily enraged, though many in the journalese-speaking fraternity believe it is simply the adjective of choice for any male under five feet six who is not legally dead. This usage reflects the continual surprise among tall journalists that short people have any energy at all. Women are rarely feisty, although they usually meet the height restriction. No journalist in America has ever referred to a six-foot male as feisty. At that height, men are "outspoken" (i.e., abusive).

In general, adjectives in journalese are as misleading as olive sizes. Most news consumers know enough to translate *developing nations* and *disadvantaged nations* back into English, but far smaller numbers know that *militant* means "fanatic," *steadfast* means "pigheaded," and *self-made* means "crooked." *Controversial* introduces someone or something the writer finds appalling, as in "the controversial Miss Fonda," and *prestigious* heralds the imminent arrival of a noun nobody cares about, as in "the prestigious Jean Hersholt Humanitarian Award."

Journalese is rich in mystic nouns: *gentrification, quichification, greenmail, watershed elections, the sleaze factor, Japanbashing, level playing fields,* the dread *T-word* (taxes), and the equally dread *L-word* (liberal). Though these nouns are patently glorious, students of the language agree that adjectives do most of the work, smuggling in actual information under the guise of normal journalism. Thus the use of *soft-spoken* (mousy), *loyal* (dumb), *high-minded* (inept), *ageless* (old), *hardworking* (plodding), *irrepressible* (insanely giddy), and *pragmatic* (morally appalling, felonious). A person who is truly dangerous as well as immoral can be described as a fierce competitor or gut fighter, and a meddling boss is a hands-on executive.

When strung together properly, innocuous modifiers can acquire megaton force. For instance, a journalist may write, "A private, deliberate man, Frobisher dislikes small talk, but can be charming when he wants to." In translation, this means "An antisocial and sullen plodder, Frobisher is outstandingly obnoxious and about as articulate as a cantaloupe." The familiar phrase "can be charming" is as central to good journalese as "affordable" is to automobile ads and "excellence" is to education reports. It indicates smoothly that Frobisher's charm production is the rare and meager result of mighty exertion, yet it manages to end the revelation about his dismal character on a plausibly upbeat note.

In journalese, folks are not grim but "grim-faced," not just plain upset but "visibly upset." *Spry* and *sprightly* refer to any senior citizen who is not in a wheelchair or a coma. Other useful adjectives include *crusty* (obnoxious), *unpredictable* (bonkers), *experienced* (over the hill), *earnest* (boring), and *authentic* (fake). The noun *stereotype* introduces the discussion of something entirely obvious which the writer intends to disparage, as in "the stereotype that little boys like to play with trucks and little girls like to play with dolls." *Life-style* has made the transition from psychobabble to journalese. Though often used incorrectly to indicate homosexuals, joggers, wheat-germ consumers, and other defiant minorities, it actually refers to any practice that makes the normal citizen's hair stand on end. The fellow who tortures iguanas in his basement has a life-style. The rest of us merely have lives.

The hyphenated modifier is the meat and potatoes of journalese. Who can forget "scandal-plagued Wedtech," "concession-prone Gorbachev," "the mop-top quartet" (the mandatory second reference to the Beatles), and the many "ill-fated" airliners, not to be confused with the "ill-fitting red wig" of Watergate fame. Murderers on death row are often saved by "eleventh-hour" reprieves, which would be somewhere between ten and eleven o'clock in English, but shortly before midnight in journalese.

Many sociologists have speculated (widely) about the love

affair between journalese-users and their hyphens. The gist of all this cerebration seems to be that the rhythm of a hyphenated modifier is soothing, like a mother's heartbeat to a babe in arms. Besides, research shows that readers cannot stand the shock of an unmodified noun, at least on first reference, any more than viewers of TV news can bear to hear Peter Jennings or Dan Rather reveal that World War III is under way without a comforting lead-in that will enable dinner to continue, though the world may not. Thus we have "Libyan-sponsored terrorism," "earthquake-ravaged Armenia," "debt-laden Brazil," and the two most popular hyphenated modifiers of the nineteen eighties, *financially-troubled* and *financially-plagued*, which can fairly be used to describe many banks, the indoor football league, the United States of America, and the entire world economy.

Many such hyphenated constructions come and go with blinding speed. "Syrian-backed PLO," once a serious contender for the hyphenation hall of fame, had to be retired when the Syrian backers began shooting at the PLO backs. Any dictator who leaves his homeland hastily, with or without his bullion and wife's shoe collection, is not running away; he is merely traveling into that famed journalistic nirvana, "self-imposed exile." In real life nobody talks that way ("Hey, Madge, did you hear? Embattled dictator Ferdinand Marcos has fled his turmoil-ridden island nation and taken up self-imposed exile on a tree-lined street in multiracial Hawaii!"), but in journalese such hyphenated chatter is considered normal.

Many meaningless adjectives, most of them hyphenated for mesmerizing effect, are permanently welded to certain nouns: *blue-ribbon panel, fact-finding mission, devout Catholic,* and *rock-ribbed Republican*. In journalese, for some reason, there are no devout Protestants or Jews, and no Democrats with strong or stony ribs. Similarly, Republicans but not Democrats may be described as staunch, which means "stiff-necked, unbending."

Like *clinically tested* and *doctor-recommended* in headache-remedy advertising, hyphenated journalese is not weakened in the slightest by the lack of any known meaning. *Wide-ranging discussions* refers to any talks at all, and *award-winning journalist* refers to any reporter, employed three or more years, who still has his own chair in a city room. A totally disappointing report, containing nothing but yawn-inducing truisms, can always be described as a "ground-breaking new study." The most exciting news on the hyphen front is that adventurous journalese-users, like late medieval theologians, are experimenting with new forms, to wit, multihyphen modifiers. So far *actor-turned-politician,* which can be found just to the left of Clint Eastwood's name in any story about Carmel, is the most beloved two-hyphen term, while *state-of-the-art* (i.e., new) is the only approved three-hyphen entry since the memorable introduction of *dyed-in-the-wool* two generations back. It is regarded as such a successful breakthrough that it may be used several times each week without reproof from any living editor.

Unbeknownst to an unsuspecting public, Boy George's drug troubles touched off a severe crisis in hyphenated journalese. How should reporters and pundits refer to the suddenly woozy singer? *Much-troubled* seemed apropos, but that adjective, like *war-torn,* is reserved for stories about the Middle East. One tabloid, apparently eager to dismiss multiproblemed George as a wanton hussy, called him "gender-confused rock star Boy George." This was a clear violation of journalese's most cherished tenet: one must, of course, do in the rich and famous, but never appear huffy in the process. *Newsweek* settled for "cross-dressing crooner," while many newspapers daringly abandoned the hyphenated tradition to label George "flamboyant," a familiar journalese word meaning "kinky" or "a person who does not have all of his or her paddles in the water."

In general, personal attacks in journalese should be accompanied by large quantities of feigned sympathy, the more unctuous the better. Thus any journalist wishing to reveal that Representative Frobisher has not been sober for ten years, will do so by respectfully hailing the poor fellow's "decade-long battle against alcohol addiction." One imaginative magazine, dishing new dirt about wife-beating in Hollywood, sadly cited one leading man's "lonely struggle against wife abuse."

Historians of journalese will agree that the first flowering of the language occurred in the description of women by splashy tabloids during the nineteen thirties and forties. In contrast to Pentagonese, which favors oxymorons *(Peacekeeper missiles, build-down),* the tabloids relied on synecdoche *(leggy brunette, bosomy blonde, full-figured redhead). Full-figured,* of course, meant "fat," and *well-endowed* meant "big-breasted," a signal to all concerned that a photo must accompany the story. *Statuesque* (too large, mooselike) and *petite* (too small, mouselike) were adjectives of last resort, meaning that the woman under discussion had no bodily parts that interested the writer. The only adjective feebler than *statuesque* and *petite* was *pert,* which indicated a plain, short woman whom the writer devoutly wished would disappear from the story.

Since it is no longer considered proper to draw the reader's attention to various protuberances and organs of the female body, journalese-users have been reduced to numbingly tame references such as *an attractive woman* (any female over fifty with no obvious facial scars) and *a handsome woman* (any woman at all). *Pert* is falling out of favor, but a formerly pert woman who is overactive or too loud as well as too short can fairly be called "perky." And of course, women are no longer blond, brunette, redheaded, or gray-haired. Any reference at all to a woman's hair color will induce a blizzard of angry feminist letters asking, in effect, why President Reagan was never described as a Clairol brunette.

Like Latin, journalese is primarily a written language, prized for its incantatory powers, and is best learned early while the mind is still supple. Every cub reporter, for instance, knows that fires rage out of control, minor mischief is perpetrated by vandals (never Visigoths, Franks, or one Vandal working alone), and key labor accords are hammered out by weary negotiators in marathon, round-the-clock bargaining sessions, thus narrowly averting threatened walkouts. The discipline required for a winter storm report is awesome. The first reference to seasonal precipitation is "snow," followed by "the white stuff," then either "it" or "the flakes," but not both. The word *snow* may be used once again toward the end of the report, directly after discussion of ice-slicked roads and the grim highway toll.

One perennial challenge in journalese is the constant need to manufacture new euphemisms for *fat*. Words such as *jolly* and *Rubenesque* have long since been understood by the public and therefore discarded. One promising recent entry, "He has a heart as big as all outdoors," while not totally successful, did manage to imply that all the rest of the gentleman's organs and limbs are quite too bulky as well. A *Washington Post* writer did better by praising a prominent woman's "Wagnerian good looks," which is far more delicate than saying, "She is not bad-looking for a massive Brunhild." This is also a sturdy example of negative journalese, which works by combining a complimentary word with an apparently innocent but actually murderous modifier. "She is still pretty," for instance, means "She is amazingly long in the tooth." The favorite female companion of a recent presidential appointee was described in the *Washington Post* as having a "blushed, taut face," which means she uses too much makeup and has had at least one face-lift.

In general, detraction in journalese must be indirect. To indicate subtle distaste for the suburbs, a *New York Times* reporter once deftly called attention to the "array of carefully trimmed lawns and neat flower beds," thus artfully suggesting compulsiveness, conformity, and a high level of intolerance for life in its hearty untrimmed state.

For years the masters of this prose cast about for a non-libelous euphemism for *mistress.* The winning entry, *great and good friend,* was invented by *Time* magazine to describe Marion Davies's relationship to William Randolph Hearst. *Constant companion* evolved later and gave way to such clunking modernisms as *roommate* and *live-in lover.* Nowadays the only sexuality about which journalese is coy tends to be homosexuality, and that is adequately covered by "He has no close female friends" or "He is not about to settle down."

Many terms in journalese come from sportswriting. *A complex, sensitive man* (lunatic) and *ebullient* (hyperactive space cadet) were developed by baseball writers confronted by a new breed of overpaid and therefore totally unpredictable jocks. *Great natural ability* is the current catchphrase for the new incompetent superstars who hit a lot of home runs but can't seem to catch a simple fly ball, throw to the right base, or correctly remember the score, the number of outs, or what day it is. Darryl Strawberry is often hailed for his great natural ability.

When ballplayers of the nineteen forties and fifties were fined for the usual excesses with women and booze, the writers dutifully reported that the penalties were for "nightclubbing." Presumably everyone knew what that meant except the nightclubbers' wives. Nowadays the vast consumption of controlled and uncontrolled substances would be covered by such time-tested circumlocutions as "He works hard and he plays hard." In sports, it is understood that all rapid declines are drug-related, and sportswriters, the original masters of journalese, are constantly casting about for nonlibelous ways of suggesting that Johnny Jumpshot is deeply in love with complex chemical compounds. The current code words are *listlessness* and *lack of concentration.* Recently, the writers have developed another un-failing indicator of drug abuse: the information that Johnny has been known to miss the team bus. This informs the astute fan that Jumpshot no longer knows where or who he is, though his body may still turn up occasionally for games. Drunken jocks, incidentally, are not listless, merely "red-eyed."

Sportswriters also taught journalese-users how to recast a boring story with exciting verbiage. Hence all the crucial is-sues, dramatic confrontations, and stunning breakthroughs, which stir and trigger almost daily. *Arguably* is the most useful adverb on the excitement frontier, because it introduces a sweeping factoid that no one will be able to check: "Frobisher is arguably the richest Rotarian living west of the Susquehanna." The runner-up adverb is *literally*, which always means "figuratively." Reforms and changes can only be "sweeping," and investigations are forever "widening," especially on days when the investigators have nothing to report, but would like a headline anyway. All arrays are bewildering, whereas contrasts are striking, except when the journalese-speaker is aware that his story is a crushingly dull one, in which case the contrast is allowed to be startling. Mounting is always followed by pressures, deficits, or concern. Slopes are slippery, precision is surgical, anyone tossed out of a job is "ousted unceremoniously," and nearly all references are "thinly veiled," unless, of course, they are "thinly disguised." Thickly disguised references are genuinely rare.

Television anchorpersons add interest to their monologues by accenting a few syllables chosen at random. Since print journalists cannot do this, except when reading aloud to spouse and family, they strive for a similar effect by using words like *crisis* and *revolution*. *Crisis* means any kind of trouble at all, and *revolution* means any kind of change at all, as in "the revolution in meat-packing." *Street value* lends dash to any drug-bust story without bearing any financial relationship to the actual value of the drugs being busted. In stories mentioning the street value of such contraband, it is generally wise to divide by ten or twelve to get the real, or nonstreet, value.

In political journalese, an officeholder who has no idea what is going on can best be described as one who "prefers to leave details to his staff." Or he can be described as having a hands-off or disengaged management style (i.e., his computer is down; he is out to lunch). Any Noriega-style gangster who runs a foreign country will usually be referred to as "strongman" until his death, and "dictator" thereafter. *Strongman,* unlike many terms in journalese, has no correlative. In the nineteen sixties, "Nicaraguan strongman Somoza" was never balanced with "Cambodian weakman Prince Sihanouk."

What to say about a public figure who is clearly bonkers? Since it is unsporting and possibly libelous to write, "Representative Frobisher, the well-known psychopath," journalese has evolved the helpful code words *difficult, intense,* and *driven.* If an article says, "Like most of us, Frobisher has his ups and downs," we are being told that Frobisher is manic-depressive. Any politician described as "suffering from exhaustion" has gone completely around the bend and is now having his mail opened for him at a discreet institution.

*Middle America* has disappeared from political journalese, for the simple reason that after eight Reagan years, America seems to be all middle with no edges. Similarly, yesterday's "radical right-winger" is today's mainstream Republican, while *unabashed* (i.e., abashed) now modifies *liberal* instead of *conservative.* Yet most political journalese is timeless. A "savvy political pro" is anyone who has lived through two or more administrations and can still get a decent table in a Washington restaurant. An elder statesman is an out-of-office politician who is senile. All seasoned reporters (old-timers) know that when two or more political appointees are fired on the same day, they need only check their calendars before tapping out "Bloody Wednesday" or "the early-Thursday-afternoon massacre." Unless, of course, *-scam* or *-gate* can be affixed to yet another noun. Each major daily has an unofficial scam-gate editor who remains ever alert for possible new coinages. A scandal involving Madison Square Garden, for instance, would be Garden-gate, and the illegal skimming of revenues could be labeled Skim-scam. *Tail-gate* has been unofficially considered for various scandals, not all of them automotive.

Political journalese also has a number of famed option plays. One man's squealer is another's whistle-blower, and Frobisher's magnificent five-point agenda can always be described as a shopping list, or worse, a wish list. My new political action group is a dedicated band of volunteers, while yours is "small but well financed" (sinister).

Political journalese, of course, requires a knowledge of sources. An unnamed analyst or observer can safely be presumed to be the writer of the article. The popular plurals *observers* and *analysts* refer to the writer and his cronies. Insiders, unlike observer-analysts, sometimes exist in the real world outside the newsroom. This, however, is never true of quotable chestnut vendors in Paris, Greenwich Village bartenders, and other colorful folk conjured up on deadline to lend a badly needed flourish to drab stories.

Almost all sources, like most trial balloonists, live in or around Washington. In order of ascending rectitude, they are: informants, usually reliable sources, informed sources, authoritative sources, sources in high places, and unimpeachable sources. Informants are low-level operatives, whose beans are normally spilled to police rather than to reporters. Informed sources, because of their informed nature, are consulted most often by sophisticated journalists. An unimpeachable source is almost always the President, with the obvious exception of Richard Nixon, who was not unimpeachable.

One of the many stressing problems in the field is writing serious articles about celebrities who recall serving in Joan of Arc's army or strolling through Iran with Jesus Christ. *Free spirit, flamboyant,* and *controversial* are not really up to the task. The journalist must avoid probing questions, such as "What does Jesus think of the Vatican's Middle East policy?" and stick to sober, respectful observations. This is best done by keeping matters vague. One *People* magazine writer, for instance, while profiling a well-known woman who has lived several times before, struck a proper tone this way: "More than most people on this earth, she has found spiritual answers."

In crime journalese, any youngster done in by a gang will turn out to be either an honor student or an altar boy. Otherwise the story will be spiked as unconventional. In any urban area, the top thug is always referred to as a "reputed mafia chieftain," or "reputed mob boss," and is generally depicted as an untutored but charismatic leader of a surprisingly efficient business operation. Except in tabloids, the chieftain's apprentice thugs are his "associates." This sort of coverage reflects the automatic respect and dignity accorded organized crime figures who know where reporters live and recognize the understandable desire of journalists everywhere to keep their kneecaps in good working order.

One inflexible rule of journalese is that American assassins must have three names: John Wilkes Booth, Lee Harvey Oswald, James Earl Ray, Mark David Chapman. This courtesy of a resonant three-part moniker is also applied to other dangerous folk. This is why the subway gunman, for the first two months of coverage, was "Bernard Hugo Goetz" to reporters who considered him a monster. Later these same scribes stripped Goetz of his Hugo, apparently on grounds that he seemed more like a malevolent wimp than an authentic three-named villain.

One subcategory of journalese, which may yet develop into a true dialect, involves the language used to indicate a powerful or celebrated person who is about to self-destruct or walk the plank. In politics, two or more stories in the same week referring to a power person as "clever," or worse, "brilliant," indicate that the end is near. Soon Mr. Scintillation will be labeled a "loose cannon" and transmute himself into a consultant, the Washington version of self-imposed exile. In business journalism, the phrase *one of the most respected managers in his field* informs knowing readers that envy is unnecessary—the respected manager is on the way out. Before long, there will be hints that his managerial ferocity is insufficient, perhaps a profile mentioning that he drinks decaffeinated coffee, loves San Francisco, or collects porcelain miniatures. This means we are less than a week from an announcement that the executive is "leaving to pursue outside interests," just like Ferdinand Marcos.

In sum, journalese is a truly vital language, the last bulwark against libel, candor, and fresh utterance. Its prestigious, ground-breaking, state-of-the-art lingo makes it arguably the most useful of tongues, and its untimely demise would have a chilling effect, especially on us award-winning journalists.

# Manila Envelopes *vs.* Kiev Chickens

**E**very sports team is supposed to have a catchy nickname, but picking a good one isn't easy. Alabama is the Crimson Tide, which sounds like a bloodbath or a serious algae problem. Notre Dame's players are ossified as the Fighting Irish, though Hibernian-American athletes are as rare at South Bend as they are on the Boston Celtics. The Oklahoma Sooners are named for land-rush cheats, who staked their claims before the legal starting time. Nebraska's Cornhuskers are the best known of a minor category of food-preparation nicknames, including the Wichita State Wheat Shockers, and the Brush (Colorado) Beet Diggers.

Nothing exposed the nickname crisis more starkly than the 1982 NCAA basketball championship game, played between the Georgetown Hoyas and the North Carolina Tar Heels. Even if you know what a hoya or a tarheel is, the only sensible strategy is to forget it. Few knew what Fort Wayne Zollner-Pistons were when a team by that name played in the National Basketball Association. (They were players owned by Fred Zollner, who also happened to own a piston factory in Fort Wayne.) The early vogue of naming a team for an owner or coach seems to have come to an end with Paul Brown, the original coach of the Cleveland Browns. Fans who found the display of ego distasteful at least were pleased that Brown's name wasn't Steinbrenner.

The Zollner-Pistons eventually became the Detroit Pistons, showing that some nicknames travel well. The Brooklyn Dodgers, named for the difficulty of evading trolley cars in the famous borough, are now the Los Angeles Dodgers, where evading mayhem on the freeways is equally hard. The name Los Angeles Lakers, however, makes no sense at all, though it once did when the team was in Minnesota, the land o' lakes. The state of Utah, with its Mormon tradition, could easily have accepted the New Orleans football team (the Saints, as in latter-day saints and saints who go marching in). Instead it got the New Orleans basketball team, now known as the Utah Jazz, which makes about as much sense as the New Orleans Tabernacle Choirs.

In general, athletic nicknames are supposed to come from two categories: animals which specialize in messy predation (lions, sharks, falcons, and so forth) or human communities famous for pillage and rapine (pirates, buccaneers, Vikings, conquistadores, bandits, raiders, et cetera). The image of mangled flesh must be evoked, but tastefully, one reason why no one has yet named a team the Massacres, or the Serial Murderers. The aim, of course, is to borrow ferocity, but there are some signs that reaction is setting in. Some years ago students at Scottsdale Community College in Arizona voted to name their team the Artichokes and picked pink and white as the team colors. Authorities balked, but three years later the students got half a loaf: the team is the Artichokes, but the colors are blue and white.

In 1986 a similar nickname struggle took place at the University of California at Santa Cruz. By a margin of 5 to 1, the student body discarded the nickname Sea Lions and decided to call the school teams the Banana Slugs, in honor of the slimy yellow gastropod that swarms over the seaside campus on rainy days. Lest the message be vague, the victorious pro-Slug students explained that the vote was fully meant to twit the "football mentality" of other colleges in the state system, whose teams go by such conventionally aggressive titles as the wildcats, toros, matadors, hornets, and warriors.

Many teams, of course, cannot fairly be accused of seeking overly aggressive names. The Maryland Terps, the Akron Zips, and the Calgary Dinosaurs do not induce terror. Nor do the New York University Violets or the Swarthmore Little Quakers. At Transylvania College, the team nickname is not the Neck-Biters, as one might expect, but the Pioneers. Women's teams are caught between the quaint feminine names of the old days (e.g., Colleens, Lassies) and the carnage-producing names of male teams. The defunct Women's Pro Basketball League had the Fillies and the Does, but leaned toward unisex names like the Pioneers, Stars, Pride, Diamonds, and Hustle. At St. John's University in Queens, where the men's basketball team is the

Redmen, the women's team is not the Squaws or the Redwomen, but the Regals. Most colleges, however, simply put the word Lady in front of the men's nickname: Lady Dragons, Lady Monarchs, and at West Point and Rutgers, the oxymoronic, and perhaps just plain moronic, Lady Knights. This process can have some odd effects. The Midwest Christian Lady Conquerors are deeply awe-inspiring, perhaps a bit more so than the Hofstra University Flying Dutchwomen or the Iowa Wesleyan Tigerettes. Conquering, by the way, is a problem at Christian colleges and high schools, since the founder of the religion came out in favor of turning the other cheek and not geopolitical mayhem. A good many Catholic high schools, plus Holy Cross College, have gotten around the problem, however, by using the nickname Crusaders, the one time-honored form of Christian slaughter. Oddly, however, the Crusaders rarely go up against a Saracen team in any remaining major sport.

In general, violent sports attract violent nicknames. Pro-basketball and pro-baseball names are fairly tame. Most of the aggressive baseball nicknames, such as Pirates and Tigers, are attached to older teams that arose when the national pastime was still a blood sport. Now that the game is played by college-trained millionaires, teams are more decorously named after seagoers and spacegoers (Mariners, Astros), birds (Blue Jays), religious figures (Angels, Padres), or a dimly remembered world's fair (Expos). While the nicknames of many older pro football teams enshrine civic boosterism (Packers, Steelers, Harvesters), the newer names include most of the violent ones. The United States Football League produced the Invaders, Maulers, Gamblers, Gunslingers, and Outlaws. As one irritated analyst put it, this group "sounds like the roster from a Hell's Angels convention."

The growth areas for professional team names are the military-industrial complex (Jets, Supersonics, Generals, Astros, Bombers, Rockets) and the more nostalgic violence of cowboys and Indians (Braves, Redskins, Chiefs, Indians, Outlaws, Rangers, Cowboys, Gunslingers, Wranglers, and Buffalo Bills). American Indians find the Indian nicknames insulting, just as most of us would doubtless fail to be amused by an All-American team in the Japanese Baseball League dubbed the Zebras for its unusual whiteskin and blackskin players. For this reason Stanford and Dartmouth have dropped the nickname Indians and now play as the Cardinals and the Big Green. St. John's has kept the nickname "Redmen," but is working hard to obscure the connection to Indians: At each game a merry mascot appears dressed in a red tuxedo.

Copycat names (Oakland Raiders, Oakland Invaders) are also popular. After the astonishing success of the New York Mets, the city had to suffer through a series of rhyming names: the football Jets, basketball Nets, the team-tennis Sets, Off-Track Betting Bets (known locally as the Debts), even some loose talk of a water polo squad to be known, inevitably, as the Wets, and a women's basketball team, the Pets. This sort of secondhand glory is an old story in sports, dating back at least to the Detroit Lions and Chicago Bears attempting to identify with the established Detroit Tigers and Chicago Cubs. Another kind of identity problem forced the Cincinnati Reds, America's oldest sports team, to change their name to the Redlegs during the height of the Cold War. One Cincinnati sportswriter objected on the grounds that since the Moscow Reds were the newcomers, they should be asked to change their name.

One trend is to name teams for malevolent forces, such as the Blast, Sting, Blizzard, or Blitz. Three team names celebrate the disasters that destroyed their home cities, the Golden Bay Earthquakes, Chicago Fire, and Atlanta (now Calgary) Flames. Such a breakthrough in reverse civic pride may yet induce other cities to celebrate their local disasters. Just think. The Boston Stranglers, the Los Angeles Smog, the Washington (D.C.) Scams, the New York Purse Snatchers.

Every now and then a real franchise attempts a punning name. A hockey team was once known as the Macon (Ga.) Whoopees, and the Los Angeles Ram cheerleaders are the Embraceable Ewes. Even the Buffalo Bills are a pun of sorts, as was the name of the late American Basketball Association St. Louis Spirits. (Get it? The Spirit of St. Louis.)

When the Washington Senators moved to the Dallas–Fort Worth area in 1972, they might have arranged to play at the Dallas Cowboys stadium in Irving, Texas. If so, the team could have glued together the names of its old and new cities, thus emerging as the Washington Irvings. No such luck. The unimaginative owners opted for the Texas Rangers. No Headless Horseman or Rip Van Winkle on the team cap, just a dull T for Texas.

Anyhow, the growing acceptance of punned nicknames opens a bright horizon for fans and players alike. Should the Norman (Okla.) squad be the Conquests or the Mailers? Could the Cincinnati Reds move to New England and become the Rhode Island Reds? When Japan finally lands a major league baseball team and hires Pete Rose as manager, why not the

Tokyo Roses? If the Minnesota Twins must relocate someday, why not to Thailand, to become the Siamese Twins? The Pittsburgh Pirates could move to the Barbary Coast or Penzance, but nowhere else. And we could save yet another famous baseball nickname if the Oakland A's moved to the Netherlands, becoming, logically, the ever-piquant Holland A's.

Spain's national team could be the Spanish I's. As astute readers will be quick to recognize, this is not just a sly reference to the popular song; it also plays off the fame of the Oakland or Holland A's (short for Athletics) with the Spanish I's (short for Inquisitions), who would torment their intradivisional rivals the Dover Souls, until finally being stopped by the Papal Bulls, formerly the Vatican Cardinals.

The Bulls would play in the Italian League along with the Venetian Blinds, Pisa Pies, Seville Barbers, and Florence Nightingales, yet another bird team to complement the Orioles, Blue Jays, and Cardinals. Exhibition games would pit the Italian League against Mediterranean Island squads such as the Malta Milks, Sicily Tysons, Rhodes Scholars, Cretan Bees, and Palma Methods, or perhaps against the easygoing resort teams from the south of France such as the Cannes Do and the Nice Guys, who, as Leo Durocher observed, finish last.

When Pete Rose leaves the U.S. to bring big-league ball to the Orient, he might bring along Dave Parker and install him in Korea as the player-manager of the Seoul Brothers. Other Asian teams include the Hong Kong Flu, Tibet Middlers (an average team), Singapore Slings, Manchurian Candidates, New Guinea Pigs, Thai Cobbs (scrappy, but not well-liked), Burma Shaves, and the Phnom Penh Pals. The China team would be the Syndrome, but Beijing would be without a team, having lost the Peking Ducks and the Peiping Toms through heedless transliteration.

Other leagues would be as follows:

Australia—Wellington Beefs, Darwin Evolvers, Sydney Greenstreets, Adelaide Laments, Perth Amboys, Tasmanian Devils, and New South Whales.

Sub-Sahara—Congo Bars, Chad Roe, Liberian Freighters, Accra Phobics, and Mali Maguires.

Middle East—Jordan Almonds, Jerusalem Artichokes, Morocco Bounders, Iran Scams, Bethlehem Stars, Tunis Fish, and Rabat Maranvilles.

India-Pakistan—Agra Cultures, Delhi Catessens, Kashmir Sweaters, Calcutta Black Holes, Bombay Doors, India Inks, Mysore Feet (exhibition games in Sri Lanka against the Colombo Detectives).

Eventually the successful Eastern European teams (Warsaw Concertos, Czech Bouncers) would create a groundswell of interest in the Soviet Union itself, giving birth to the Moscow Mules, Gorky Parks, Georgia O'Keeffes, Brest Beaters, and Yalta Agreements, dubbed the "Sellouts" by the New York *Daily News.*

With proper controls over the spread of nicknames around the world, someday we will undoubtedly see some magical matchups. Opening Day, 1999: Kiev Chickens at Delhi Catessens; Persian Pen-Letters at Manila Envelopes, Holland A's at Canberra Sauces . . .

# Womenspeak
# *vs.* Mentalk

**Ralph:** Wanda, look at this phone bill! Has AT&T misplaced some zeroes, or did you spend all last month jabbering with far-off friends?

**Wanda:** None of the above, Ralph. But I must admit you have put your finger on yet another important sexual difference. Women spend far more time on the telephone than men do, even when they have relatively little to say.

**Ralph:** I am a clever husband, dearest. Do not try to get around me by taking my role in this script.

**Wanda:** I wouldn't think of it, Ralph. Studies show that males are brief, almost abrupt, on the phone. Once in a while you all blab endlessly, telling knock-knock jokes and so forth, but on the whole, men use the phone like a telegram. This may be because you like to make a show of being terribly busy, or because, by female standards, you are all emotionally constricted. Probably some combination of the two.

**Ralph:** Getting to the point is not a character flaw, dearest. Why is it that the less a woman has to say, the longer she will stay on the phone to say it?

**Wanda:** Once again there is a rough truth behind your insult, pugnacious one. Researchers Mark Sherman and Adelaide Haas of the State University of New York at New Paltz found that women are almost three times as likely as men to make a phone call when they have nothing special to say. Women use the phone to work at friendship. You shouldn't feel bad when you start blustering about this, by the way. In her book *Intimate Strangers,* therapist Lillian Rubin says the husband's anger about his wife's use of the phone is absolutely standard in the American household. She thinks that men feel so abandoned when their women are on the phone that it reawakens the male's dependence on Mommy. Don't bother to protest, Ralph. I don't believe it either.

**Ralph:** This conversation is an amazement, Wanda. Do you intend to speak all my lines?

**Wanda:** Unfeminine, isn't it? Let us plunge on. We know that men hate to talk about emotions and the psyche. That's why psychology is regarded as a low-prestige, "female" occupation at many colleges, unless psychology is defined there as the tormenting of imprisoned rats. We know that males are far more likely than females to talk about sports and politics, and would practically fall silent nine-tenths of the time if those subjects were out of bounds.

**Ralph:** How about those Tigers? A helluva team.

**Wanda:** We know that women work harder at conversation. They ask far more questions, partly to keep the conversation going, partly to placate the male, who tends to control the conversation.

**Ralph:** You mean like I'm controlling this one?

**Wanda:** A California researcher taped fifty-two hours of conversation by three middle-class couples and found that women brought up twice as many topics as men but that males controlled the talks by vetoing subjects they didn't want to discuss. The men achieved this, the clever dears, by grunts and long silences. Out of desperation, the females asked three times as many questions as men and started larding their comments with the interjection *you know.* Having a civil conversation with your average male is like playing tennis with a partner who's asleep.

**Ralph:** Certainly this approaches the brink of insensitivity, dearest one. Last week when you were puzzled about what went wrong between you and Doris, didn't I pitch right in and suggest that you call her up and confront her?

**Wanda:** Very manly and direct, Ralph. And all wrong. Sherman and Haas say this is a standard husband-wife conversation that ends with an angry wife. The woman states an emotional problem, and one tenth of a second later the man says, "Here's what you do. . . ." That's not why wives raise these issues with husbands. We want emotional support and a good listener, not instant cracker-barrel advice.

**Ralph:** Next time you have a wrenching problem, count on me to sit around helpfully saying, "Hmmm." Wanda, I ask you, is there no hope for men?

**Wanda:** Probably not in our lifetime. In her book *Women and Men Speaking,* sociolinguist Cheris Kramarae reports that 466 men and women termed male speech "forceful, dominating, boastful, and authoritarian." Female speech was characterized by both sexes as "friendlier, gentler, faster, more emotional, enthusiastic, and trivial."

**Ralph:** We can always try harder to be trivial. How do you like my new socks? Aren't they darling?

**Wanda:** Most of these studies conclude that dominance runs through male conversation with women. The kibbutzim of Israel were supposed to embody the ideal of sexual equality. But anthropologist Lionel Tiger, in research for his book *Women in the Kibbutz,* found that men talked for three-quarters of the total time at town meetings. The only time women talked more than men was when the topic was curtain-making. The point is—

**Ralph:** What else do we do wrong?

**Wanda:** You interrupt. Studies at the University of California at Santa Barbara show that men interrupt women all the time. When two men or two women are talking, interruptions are about equal. But when a man talks to a woman, he makes ninety-six percent of the interruptions. But—

**Ralph:** These people have nothing better to do than study interruptions?

**Wanda:** —but women make "retrievals" about one third of the time. You know, they pick up where they left off after the man—

**Ralph:** Surely not all men are like that, Wanda.

**Wanda:** —cuts in on what they were saying. It seems—

**Ralph:** Speaking as a staunch supporter of free speech for women, I officially deplore this, Wanda.

**Wanda:** (Sigh.) I know, Ralph. I know.

# "We're the Folks at Unitox"

The Ford Motor Company once considered more than 6,000 possible names for a new series of cars, including Zip and Drof (Ford spelled backwards). As part of the search, David Wallace of the Ford Special Products Division carried on a long correspondence with the poet Marianne Moore. After a few throat-clearing mumbles about "the fragile meaning of words," Wallace got right to the point: the name of the new car should be pure verbal magic, conveying "some visceral feeling of elegance, fleetness, advanced features and design," one that "flashes a dramatically desirable picture in people's minds."

The poet's response was zestfully misguided. In a blizzard of spirited notes, she suggested the Ford Silver Sword, Hurricane Hirundo, Mongoose Civique, Anticipator, Pastelogram,

Dearborn Diamante, Turcotinga, the Resilient Bullet, the Intelligent Bullet, and the Intelligent Whale. Out of politeness or fright, Wallace and his minions seemed unable to stanch this creative torrent. Almost a year after Ms. Moore's final proposal (her last stab was Turtletop), Wallace broke the bad news. Though "it fails somewhat of the resonance, gaiety, and zest we were seeking," the new car would be called the Edsel.

A list of suggestions from Shakespeare himself would not have saved the Edsel, the Dearborn Disaster of its era, but at least Ford had the corporate presence of mind to ignore a poet's chatter about civic-minded ferrets and high-IQ bullets. Nowadays executives who are eager to name products or rename companies seem infinitely more suggestible. Someone actually paid good money to be known as Allegis, Unisys, and Trinova.

While an uncomprehending nation tries to cope, corporate America is shedding dowdy smokestack names in favor of spiffy space-age ones. The American Can Company has become Primerica, United States Steel has compressed itself into USX, Massey-Ferguson is Varity, what is left of International Harvester is now Navistar, and a company named Bradford National is, for some undisclosed reason, Fidata, which many will swear is the name of a minor animal in the movie *Pinocchio.*

To nearly universal mirth, United Air Lines emerged wondrously as the butterfly Allegis before corporate breakup and a great deal of hooting forced it back into the cocoon again as just plain United Air Lines. Like Ms. Moore's Turcotinga (short for turquoise cotinga, a tropical bird) Allegis is a lilting nonword formed by collapsing two real words, *allegiance* and *aegis,* both meant to evoke toasty feelings of loyalty and rightful jurisdiction in unwary consumers. But these are misty matters. Allegis might just as frequently have reminded people of allegations, all legislators, or allergies. Donald Trump, who avoids the entire problem by putting his name on everything he owns, won the surprised assent of the public by observing that Allegis sounds like "the next world-class disease."

For a fee that can stretch into the high six figures, corporate identity consultants such as NameLab and Lippincott & Margulies will instruct their computers to expectorate a few thousand word bits, arranged and rearranged for mesmerizing effect. Navistar, besides echoing the rhythm of Harvester, can evoke anyone who navigates by stars, from the Magi to Columbus, as well as Roger Staubach, Dave Robinson, and other jocks who starred for Navy.

One trend is to make the new company sound like a cancer cure currently available only in Uruguay: Enron, Concor, Ephemeron, Enco, and so forth. Another is to follow Xerox and Exxon by inserting an $x$ or two for mystifying effect: Xylex, Xelex, Xidex, USX, Nynex. When Primerica was chosen by American Can, ten of the fifteen computer-generated runner-ups were $x$ names. $X$ products and companies have always seemed to do well, from Tampax to Kleenex, and Wall Street seems to consider $x$ a futuristic letter. Then, too, the $x$ sound, and the $k$ sound imbedded in it, are the staples of male cursing and therefore bear a high degree of awesomely aggressive management machismo. The same is true of the $k$ and $q$ names, and the many techs: Suntek, Compaq (ye olde spelling of the abbreviated computer-pack), Amtrak (trains) and its sound-alike Armtek (rubber).

Another great frontier is names for new cars. With cars, one trend is to take a perfectly ordinary English word and lop off a few letters for effect: Accura, Festiva, et cetera. Mercedes-Benz and BMW seem to do nicely without names like Carniva, Punctua, or in fact without any names at all. NameLab dreamed up an arrestingly mundane name for a no-nonsense Nissan car: Sentra, which is meant to evoke *sentry* (watchfulness) and *centrist* (stable, not extreme). This is one step up from naming a car the Nissan Dullsville. If bad times are truly looming, customers can always hunker down in their Sentras, the ideal vehicle for cautious and vigilant moderates.

One pitfall of a new name is that it can sound negative or obscene in a foreign tongue. Chevy's Nova translates as "does not go" in Spanish. Enco, a proposed name rejected in favor of Exxon, means "stalled car" in Japanese. (Detroit can only wish.) Enteron, one of the cancer-cure names proposed for HNG/Internorth, turned out to be an existing medical term for the alimentary canal.

When all imagination fails, companies can always arrive at a new name by collapsing the old one. A generation ago, First National City Bank pointed the way by contracting into Citibank. After merging, the Dutch holding companies Ago and Ennia scrambled all the letters of both names, threw away three, and became Aegon. Bucking the trend, Aegon failed to use a computer or pay $50,000. An employee thought it up and got a few shares of stock for his noncomputerized effort.

There's an even cheaper way to do it, of course. If you don't like Smucker's or Smith Brothers and wish to burnish the corporate image, you can skip the year-long five-hundred-thousand-dollar search and just play around for twenty minutes with a bunch of surefire word bits: *prime, data, fid, ico, uni, tele, comput, tech, tek, con, ron, tron, en, am, dex, paque* or *pack, inter, trans, xe,* and *star.* These modern corp-o-bits can be combined at random for a terrific new name at very little cost. Uniteletrans, for instance, Compudatago, Xeronico, or Intertechamericon. Anyone who can play Scrabble (Skrablexico?) can certainly do this. Let us say a new name is being sought by Toxic Waste Inc., an old-line firm famous for swift nighttime disposal of chemicals in underdeveloped sections of New Jersey. Chances are the computer would suggest Uni-Tox, Toxico, Toxeron, DTX, Toxistar, or Toxamerica.

Saving all that money is a worthwhile reform for corporate America. Another is simply to forget the whole idea of reaching for a dazzling macho moniker, and just put the energy into making products that work. Chances are that the Edsel would have been a turkey even if the chrome said Turcotinga.

# FUMBLING
# AROUND THE
# HOUSE

# Why Men
# Don't Do
# Chores

**Wanda:** How about doing the kitchen floor, Ralph?

**Ralph:** It's okay with me, dearest. I'll be in the TV room eagerly awaiting the completion of this all-important task.

**Wanda:** You misconstrue my meaning, stationary one. I mean, since you are the nominal codirector of this household, how about actually levitating out of your comfy chair and seizing a mop? It's the long-handled instrument with the stringy stuff at the end.

**Ralph:** Alas, I'm not into waxy yellow buildup, dearest, and the floor looks plenty clean to me. Besides, you and I know that a crucial kitchen floor is no place for on-the-job training—I'd probably screw it up. What if I took out the garbage, fixed the boiler, or used my sheer animal strength to open a tight jar of olives—something manly like that.

**Wanda:** These are tasks of simple maintenance, not tests of your manhood, Ralph. We both have jobs. Why should I do all the housework?

**Ralph:** That would be grossly unfair, my pet. Just imagine the burden on you if I didn't help clear the table, grill the hamburgers all summer, clean out the garage each spring, and perform the myriad chores associated with the concerned husband in a contemporary two-career family.

**Wanda:** Ralph, apart from your arduous job of watching the TV all the time—so that no one will steal it—you do around ten percent of the work in this house, about average for the American male, I guess. You do one sweaty job a month, chop down a tree or something, then sink back in post-Rambo exhaustion while I log forty or fifty hours each week cleaning, shopping, doing laundry, and looking after the kids. If I ask you to help, you either develop a trick knee or some incredible sports event is on the tube. I suppose this is fair?

**Ralph:** As the resident male feminist, I want you to know that Alan Alda and I are in full agreement that men should do half the chores.

**Wanda:** That's great, Ralph. It's nice to know I have your full theoretical support while I'm doing the laundry and you're watching the national bottlecap-bending championship, live from Fresno. Men have learned to make the right noises about helping, but women are still doing almost all the housework. A Virginia Slims poll of women showed that chores are evenly divided in only fifteen percent of American households. Economist Heidi Hartman calls the male contribution around the house "small, selective, and unresponsive," and she suggests that husbands may require more maintenance than they perform, making them a net drain on the family's resources. Various surveys show that working women do between sixty-seven and ninety percent of all household chores. Husbands don't even help out when they lose their jobs. They generally sit around all day, letting the wife do the chores when she gets home.

**Ralph:** Pardon me, dearest—haven't you just escalated the kitchen floor into a national crisis?

**Wanda:** Not yet, Ralph. You may think evading chores is kind of cute, but Sylvia Hewlett, in her book *A Lesser Life,* argues that the male refusal to help out is wearing women out and hurting the careers of working mothers—the less work men do, the more women have to cut corners at work to manage kids and household, thus risking chances for promotion. Actually there's a guerrilla war going on in the two-career home. In their book *American Couples,* sociologists Pepper Schwartz and Philip Blumstein report that the more housework men do, the more they fight about it and help sour the relationship, just like you slyly threatened to mess up the floor if I made you mop it. It either makes women feel guilty for asking, or makes them do all the work themselves to avoid trouble.

**Ralph:** But surely things are improving as more men see the light.

**Wanda:** Actually, they're not. The depressing thing is that younger men seem just as recalcitrant as dedicated codgers like yourself. A national poll called *The Ethan Allen Report on the Family*, brought the bad news that younger couples battle the most about housework. Nearly half of dual-career families with children said housework is a source of conflict. Surveys show that men are doing slightly more housework than they did ten years ago, but when you figure how many married women have poured into the work force in that time, the increase is pitiful.

**Ralph:** Amazing how you happen to have all these statistics at hand when we have an impromptu argument, dearest. Any stats in there about the degree of male enthusiasm for doing every chore the female way?

**Wanda:** And what exactly is the female way, pugnacious one?

**Ralph:** A path fraught with obsession. Every time I thoughtfully load the dishwasher or tuck in a sheet, it turns out I did it wrong. Multiply this by a million and you have a portrait of the modern househusband's predicament. Who wants to be measured against some astonishing yet secret female ideal? We just want to get the job done.

**Wanda:** I know, Ralph. Every time you do a fifteen-minute job, it takes me twenty minutes to clean up after you.

**Ralph:** If your standards were a tad lower, we would have no argument, beloved polemicist. Remember, men did not come to rule the world, and thus launch the worldwide conspiracy against women, by using all their spare time polishing the ceiling or getting up early to vacuum before the maid comes. This is my only qualm about women in the army, by the way. In combat, your basic woman soldier would shoot two of the enemy, throw down her rifle, rush over, pack up and store the bodies neatly, vacuum the site, then run back to her foxhole, ready to resume firing in a properly clean setting.

**Wanda:** We have come a long way in this little discussion, Ralph. Am I correct in assuming that you have just offered to do a first-rate job on the kitchen floor if I promise not to oversee you or comment on the quality of the work?

**Ralph:** Bingo, dearest. When a woman treats her hubby like an underling in need of supervision, studies show that she's really declaring housework to be her responsibility. It isn't just yours, you know. Phil Donahue and I agree on that.

**Wanda:** Here's the mop, unsupervised one.

**Ralph:** Great. I'll find the Windex myself.

# Some
# Assembly
# Required

It is Christmas Eve, and you think all the work is done. The children are more or less nestled all snug in their beds. You have wasted the mandatory twenty minutes untangling the tree lights, which someone else has always put away sloppily the year before, and you have endured the annual ritual of straightening the tree carefully, with each leg of the fiendishly designed three-legged base taking its turn to fall out onto the floor. The presents are under the tree. You are under the impression that it is time to relax, when your spouse utters the dread sentence, "Dear, we have to put some of these toys together."

Childlessness has many obvious advantages. One is that you need not spend $200,000 to send anyone to college, or contribute a similar sum to the retirement fund of a stranger who has decided to become a pediatrician. But the principal advantage of the nonparental life-style is that on Christmas Eve, you need not be struck dumb by the three most terrifying words that the government allows to be printed on any product: "Some assembly required." Heavy of heart, you know exactly what the words mean. Some sadist across the Pacific has just invented yet another toy that you will never be able to put together.

Let's say you buy your child one of the new killer toys, Captain Ego. Since you probably watch fewer than a thousand hours a year of Saturday-morning television, you foolishly think that the famously violent action-figure will simply pop out of a box, staring at you balefully with his one good eye. This is all wrong. Nowadays killer dolls are usually made up of fourteen or fifteen toy automobiles, which a stupefied parent must assemble into a plausible mass murderer sometime before dawn on Christmas Day. No one knows why death-dealing humanoids are composed of multicolored cars. Maybe they do it that way so that the beloved slaughterer can escape in various directions after dispatching his daily quota of the innocent. Your job is not to judge the Captain, but simply to put him together before you lose control and join him in his customary rage.

You approach this logically. Obviously the red car over there is the laser gun, and the blue one has a catalytic converter that folds down to become the killer's head, but how do they all connect? Since you are impatient and already mildly annoyed at having to cope with a tiny murderer's bodily problems on the eve of a major holiday, you are anxious to get it over with. So you make the first of the two major toy-assembly mistakes known to mankind: you refuse to read the instructions. This is liberating, in a way. You are on your own, just like the Captain, disdaining the rules and explanations of rational society. Surely any fool can put a vigilante doll together and have him clumping around on his brand-new Toyotas in no time at all. But, alas, the movable parts slide in and out of the various autos, but never grab one another to form one unitary serial-killer, so you grow frustrated. You just can't figure it out. And so, in your perfectly understandable weakness, you make the second of the great toy-assembly errors: you read the instructions.

Ten or fifteen years ago, reading the instructions was not really an option. This is because all Japanese toymakers of the period insisted on having the Japanese instructions translated first into a little-known Portuguese dialect by an Urdu-speaking Zulu, and then into something vaguely resembling English by a wayward Mongolian folk-humorist who had once seen an American movie. Thus "Insert Tab (a) into Slot (b)" always came out as "Introject initial protruder (a) at approximately aperture (2)."

The final paragraphs of such instructions were works of high comic art. Often they dispensed with verbs altogether. Occasionally there was a sober final instruction in fear-inducing capital letters that usually said something like "Attention: recall that transiform must be mogrified before Step Three or small child may unduly perish!" These instructions, intended to convince America that Japan was a fun-loving backward nation that would never amount to much, were never as richly amusing on Christmas Eve as they were when you told friends about them a couple of days later. Toys, like life, were simpler then, so parents muddled through. All of us knew that Tab (a) would definitely go into Slot (b), but only at the exact instant that Tab (x), by way of compensation, flew out of Slot (y), forcing us to break off a few aperture-introjections and end up using a roll or two of tape to hold the fool transiform together just long enough to get through the opening ceremonies of Christmas morning. The important thing was to retain composure and paddle back to the warm holiday spirit. So what if all the toys listed a bit to one side? They were obviously overengineered anyway, and if you had an axle or two left over, you just kicked them over there behind the tree and Junior never noticed.

Today these time-honored methods are considered slap-dash, partly because the Japanese, in one of their famous economic gambles, decided to hire English-speaking translators. Other Asian toymakers did the same, so now American parents have the option of being totally confused by instructions in their own tongue: "Take the decibar and connect it through the assembly aperture to the pendant rod bracket flange of the left ratchet mount, using continelle bolts and nut retainers, as shown." The "as shown" is a nice touch. Just when you hit a sentence that no living human can follow, they throw in "as shown" to indicate suavely that almost any dunderhead should be able to put the toy together in a jiffy by flicking a single casual glance at the miraculously clear illustration. The illustration, of course, looks like a drug-induced hallucination of the toy flying apart, with helpful arrows rapidly fleeing from the multiform modal chassis.

Let's say you keep your temper long enough to put the toy together. At this point you will come upon an instruction, deliberately put at the end, that will force you to take the whole thing apart: "Warning: all shaft springs, before connection to right drive slip coil units, must be rubbed counterclockwise with clear detergent or toy will self-destruct during second use." Among savvy parents, this is known as the time bomb at the end of the instructions. A simple corollary of the time-bomb rule is that wherever you start, it's the wrong place, because something else has to be done first. Step One, which many parents insist on thinking of as the first step, tells you to put the pedals together, attaching them to previously constructed pedal rod unit. Naturally, the pedal rod unit cannot be put together until the shaft spin-out retaining lever of the central steering assembly is built around it, and so forth. The gist of this is that if you start with Step One, you are beginning too late in the instructions and will never finish.

Still, putting toys together can be achieved with deep inner peace if you are willing to understand and adapt the forces at work in the toy culture. Here are some of the things you must know:

1) Whatever goes wrong, it's your fault. This principal can hardly be overstressed. A friend of mine, not heeding this rule, once called the manufacturer of a toy to complain. The spokesman said that only foolish innocents pay attention to the instructions, which, he explained patiently, made no sense to him at all.

2) If the only screwdriver you own is a Phillips, the instructions will require a regular flatheaded screwdriver, and vice versa. Similarly, if you own every type of battery sold in America, the small print will inform you that the toy takes the rare seven-and-a-half-volt prismatic battery, available by mail from Vienna in packages of thirteen.

3) If the instructions say that seventeen parts are con-

tained in the parts envelope, the package will actually contain sixteen or eighteen. The toymakers who include the extra part believe it is that last straw that will make the parent break, fearing he or she has truly messed up and left out a crucial screw. The toymakers who leave you one part short also hope to break your spirit, but wish to save two or three cents while doing so.

4) Since instructions are not meant to be understood, as parents get more sophisticated, the toymakers are under constant competitive pressure to raise the murkiness level of the company prose. This means that no matter how well you educate your children, they will not be any better at this than you are. Some Christmas Eve in the year 2010, they, too, will be scratching their heads, possibly over the assembly instructions for the self-actuating quarks that your grandchildren plan to use on the newly geriatric Captain Ego, slaughterer of millions. This is comforting and important to a parent's sense of continuity. As your grown children stand there in midquandary, you can always lean back, sip your eggnog, and suavely mention that in your day, parents always began with a good detergent bath for the unassembled shaft springs and continelle nut retainers. But then you smile and think, it's none of your business now.

# Save Your Marriage, Just $19.95

**Ralph:** Something's gone wrong in this bookstore, Wanda. I can't seem to find the Personal Growth section. Wasn't it over here between Gay Studies and Amatory Methodologies?

**Wanda:** This is the late nineteen eighties, Ralph. They took out Personal Growth. Some of the space went to Money Management—those five aisles over there—and the rest went to this new section, Interpersonal Realization.

**Ralph:** Interpersonal Realization?

**Wanda:** Books on how to save your marriage. On the right are all the books on how marriage is happy and great, and you have to stick with it. On the left are the books on how marriage can be pretty rough and horrible, but you have to stick with it.

**Ralph:** It's heartwarming to see the old verities rendered trendy, my love. But what do these books actually say?

**Wanda:** Most of them you would probably dismiss as inspirational, hardhearted one. *Married People: Staying Together in the Age of Divorce* says you must accept change and your partner's limitations, that there is no formula, no single recipe, for a successful marriage.

**Ralph:** Life has no easy answers, dearest, but often we must publish anyway. What else is in these books?

**Wanda:** A lot of them talk about getting the right "comfort zone." That's the amount of emotional space we need. *Thank God, It's Monday! or How to Prevent Success from Ruining Your Marriage* says that a husband "may feel his wife's comfort zone is too close for comfort." And Carol Botwin, author of *Is There Sex After Marriage?*, says that when someone steps too far into our comfort zone, we withdraw, sometimes sexually.

**Ralph:** What are sex books doing here? Don't they belong over there in Amatory Methodologies?

**Wanda:** Not anymore, Ralph. These are different—they go in the sexual subsection of Interpersonal Realization. For example, this one by Dagmar O' Connor—*How to Make Love to the Same Person for the Rest of Your Life*— is not one of those grunt-and-grope books, like *The Joy of Sex*. As it says on the flap, it's "the book for the Age of Commitment." It's about intimacy and building a great marriage by finding lifelong sexual excitement with your mate.

**Ralph:** So the sex books that save your marriage are the high-toned ones that don't go into all that messy detail?

**Wanda:** Unless imaginative sexuality is necessary to save the marriage. *Keep the Home Fires Burning: How to Have an Affair with Your Spouse* is open-minded about marriage saving, but it frowns on sex that involves welts and bruises.

**Ralph:** Let's get back to the comfort zone, my beloved. Would it be fair to say that women, the market for these books, are interested in more emotion, conversation, involvement, and that men are remote cold-hearted brutes who slump in an easy chair each night, ignoring the inner plight of the little woman?

**Wanda:** Correcto, Ralph. One book talks about a husband who says "I love you" only when he is naked and horizontal. Another claims that men want to hear "I love you" only once, whereas women want to hear it more than once. It recommends that men say "I love you" three times in a row. That advice appears in *The Silicon Syndrome: How to Survive a High-Tech Relationship*, by Jean Hollands, but it's really too hard-hitting a book to discuss with you, intolerant one.

**Ralph:** Stonehearted hubbies can take anything, Wanda. Fire away.

**Wanda:** Well, *Syndrome* is about how to hold a marriage together in Silicon Valley, the natural home of cold, remote engineer-scientist males. Most men are afraid to show their feelings. The Silicon man doesn't seem to have any. When the wife wants to make some emotional connection, like during a crisis, Silicon man runs up to his brain and sits there awhile.

**Ralph:** Surely this is warm jocularity.

**Wanda:** Hollands is serious, and she says Silicon man is everywhere. Her book lists a lot of ways you can chop through the male ice. One of the best is to say, "I know that my personality is hard on you." Rapid meltage occurs so regularly that the author calls the sentence "the magic words." She also recommends a verbal exercise for expressing resentment. One partner says, "I resent that you . . ." and then expresses the complaint. The other then responds with three set comments: "Thank you for sharing that. Your saying so may not change my behavior. I'm not going to defend myself."

**Ralph:** I've heard better dialogue in Arnold Schwarzenegger movies.

**Wanda:** Wisecracks make you ineligible for rehabilitation, Ralph. These are sharing exercises, and a lot of the books have them. For instance, *Second Marriage: Make It Happy! Make It Last!* recommends the two-question rule in marital communication.

**Ralph:** Just what marriage needs, Wanda, more rules. Okay how does it work?

**Wanda:** Let's say I come home and say, "What a day I had!" Nine times out of ten you will say, "Your day! Wait till you hear about my day!" That's no good. What you have to do is ask two concerned questions and recapitulate the emotions I am expressing. It's supposed to go something like this: "What a day I had!" "I figured something was wrong when you weren't home at six. What happened?" "My boss is putting a lot of pressure on me." "You sound really upset. What kind of pressure is he putting on you?" And so on.

**Ralph:** Gee, that's great, Wanda. With these books you can conduct entire marital conversations all by yourself. Just think you can have a meaningful dialogue, in a marriage-saving manner, even before I get home.

**Wanda:** Maybe you'd better read the book on saving your second marriage, Ralph. You don't seem to be doing too well with this one.

**Ralph:** Sensitivity is important in a good marriage, my pet. Here I stand, vertical and clothed, saying I love you, I love you, I love you. That's three times. And I ask two caring questions: Why don't we go home? And what's for dinner?

**Wanda:** Par for the course. When you are through babbling, Ralph, look for me over there in Divorce Studies.

# Manly about the House

On Labor Day I smashed my left hand playing middle-aged softball in the Hamptons. The worst part is that we had just rented a heavy-pressure hose to bleach seven years' worth of mold off our cedar shingle house and the job had to be done that day. ("Don't let this hose get away from you—it can tear the flesh right off your arm," the rental agent said gravely, obviously aware that he was dealing with a macho kind of guy.)

Actually, I did let the hose get away from me. As I fumbled with it, one-armed, but clearly in complete control, I heard my wife say in mildly exasperated tones, "Here, let me have it." While I glanced around, fearing the sight of neighbors clapping their foreheads in horror, Mrs. Rambo proceeded to hoist the heavy hose and detoxify our entire dwelling without tearing any noticeable flesh from either arm.

My first thought was to run and hide the chain saw. After all, my wife had just violated one of the best-known rules of marital harmony, i.e., all outdoor tasks except gardening are the proper province of the husband. Males chop wood, scramble up ladders, fix gutters, poison moles, and bury decomposing raccoons. Women do the indoor stuff, except for building bookcases and opening tight pickle jars.

This was the prefeminist division of duties around the average American house. You may have noticed that it is also, roughly, the postfeminist division. Nowadays women tend to open their own jars and try a few traditional male jobs, just as men tend to do a bit of halfhearted housecleaning. But on the whole the division of tasks established by Tarzan and Jane is still with us. You rarely see men picking the wallpaper border or women fixing the boiler and jumping under the Buick to check the twin-bar suspension.

The reason for this is genetic. Competent genealogists tell me I come from two hundred generations of males who have been unable to operate a vacuum properly. Reality crushed my totally nonsexist illusions on this point when my wife left one week on a business trip. Since she cares deeply about a clean household and coming back to freshly vacuumed rooms, I vowed to meet her ozone-level standards. Taking care to insert the hose into what I felt sure was the correct end of the vacuum, I set out to whoosh up every speck of dirt on the premises. I did this over and over each day. When my wife returned she said kindly, "Everything looks great. All it needs now is a good vacuuming."

In place of the missing vacuuming gene, males have a bizarre pre-party gene which one day will probably be removed routinely through *in utero* surgery. This is the gene that forces the male to undertake irrelevant construction tasks like building bookcases and resanding hardwood floors just before thirty guests are due to arrive. I do this all the time. To my amazement, my wife sometimes grows irritated, as if I had some sort of control over this obviously instinctual masculine behavior.

Women, on the other hand, have extra bits of DNA, such as the one which pushes them to get up early and clean before the maid arrives. (What would the male equivalent be: reroofing the house before the roofer comes?) I myself have recently established the existence of yet another unsuspected female gene. It occurred when my wife, who has just taken on a big new job and always has a hundred or so other projects going at once, said last week, "Let's paint the pantry. Pantries are important."

This pantry gene is totally unknown in men. I have never met a male anywhere who is willing to say aloud that pantries really matter. I myself would be more likely to embroider the likeness of Mrs. Millard Fillmore on the bottom of our guest-room boxspring than even think about freshening up the coat of paint which is apparently inadequate for our overpampered pantry. To begin with, very few of our friends spend much time in this room. Those who do are probably too distracted by the riotous colors of American food products to complain much about our inferior pantry care.

The only cleaning and maintenance jobs men love are outdoorsy, macho, and preferably easy. So give me back my water cannon and let me spray the mold off my cedar shingles. This is man's work: it's over in an hour or two, doesn't have to be redone for another seven years, and involves no vacuuming or other cleanup. Best of all it's the ideal chore to while away those idle moments just before the annual lawn party.

# Legal
# Valentines

**Wanda:** Got a question for you, Ralph. Jacalyn Barnett is an attorney who recommends "highlighting the legal consequences of love." What do you suppose she is talking about?

**Ralph:** About two hundred an hour in paternity-suit litigation, my pet, maybe three hundred if she's bright enough to specialize in rock singers.

**Wanda:** Outstandingly wide of the mark, Ralph. Actually, it's marriage contracts—prenuptial agreements, if you will. Barnett is head of the matrimonial department at a large New York law firm and she calls them "legal valentines" that can be "loving and protective documents."

**Ralph:** Lawyers are justly famous for their romantic view of the world, Wanda. I grant you that nothing is more exhilarating than preparing for marriage and divorce at the same time. But these contracts are old stuff. Why bring them up now?

**Wanda:** There's been an exciting breakthrough in prenuptials and even postnuptials, Ralph. In the old days, people just protected themselves financially in case of divorce. Now couples are adding life-style clauses. Sociologist Lenore Weitzman, author of *The Marriage Contract,* calls them "blueprints for behavior." For instance, a contract may stipulate that the husband agrees to do half the vacuuming and child-rearing or take the wife out to dinner at least twice a week for the length of the marriage.

**Ralph:** If I sign up for Chinese once a week, is it okay with Lenore if I legally get hungry again in an hour?

**Wanda:** Then there are the sexual provisions. One contract specified that the husband was allowed to fool around only when he was out of town, never in his home city. Some agreements say the husband or wife get a night or two out each week with no questions asked, and many contracts insist that the bride and groom detail their sexual life histories before the wedding.

**Ralph:** You can never start recriminations too early in a marriage, dearest.

**Wanda:** All right, Ralph. Tell me your problem with this.

**Ralph:** Marriage contracts for people who don't want to be married are a marketing triumph, my sweet. Imagine a fellow's legal embarrassment when he finds himself curled up with a bimbo in a Minneapolis hotel and his contract says he can only cheat in St. Paul. Maybe he should phone his wife's lawyer for an easement. Pushing back the frontier of the preposterous is arduous labor, Wanda, and I often wonder why lawyers and sociologists have to shoulder so much of the burden.

**Wanda:** Don't blame them, Ralph. Couples want these agreements. In fact, some stick-in-the-mud lawyers and family counselors don't really approve. Robert Herman, an attorney in Rochester, calls life-style clauses "an awful waste of money," and Don Smith, a California counselor, says "It goes from the silly to the stupid." He says he has helped couples negotiate "everything from who's going to pick up the doggie poo to the usual stuff on feeding the kids and doing the dishes."

**Ralph:** Look at the advantages, dearest. Due to this brilliant legal breakthrough, faulty dog-poop removal may be proper grounds for divorce.

**Wanda:** Not really, Ralph. Only the financial provisions seem to be enforceable. Barnett drew up a clause for a man who wanted his wife to remain slim, so the marriage contract said she would pay a fine if she gained weight, refundable upon weight loss. It's probably legally binding. Weitzman wants to see "liquidated damages"—if the hubby is supposed to fix the plumbing and doesn't, he would have to pay the value of that service as a fine.

**Ralph:** It might be easier to remain single and just hire the help, beloved wife. For one thing, your plumber can't fine you if you develop crow's feet or receding gums. Unless, of course, his work contract has a life-style clause prepared by Jacalyn Barnett.

**Wanda:** It's not as dumb as you think, my naysaying husband. People have higher expectations of marriage than they used to, and the attempt to list some of these expectations is all to the good. It wouldn't be such a bad idea for us to work out a contract, Ralph.

**Ralph:** Trippingly told, my sweet. Okay, in the absence of a pettiness advisor, let's hammer out our own contract.

**Wanda:** You go first.

**Ralph:** Okay. I want you to respect my two favorite hobbies— watching TV and resting. You will owe me five big ones if you ever criticize Frank Sinatra, serve sodium-free potato chips, or bring into this house any book written by a seagull or Leo Buscaglia. Outside of that, I'm easy. Of course, if I stick flamingos in the front yard, defend secondhand smoke, or say something coarse about the snail darter, I'll pay you. I will agree never to go bald. And naturally, I expect you to remain wrinkle-free and wasp-waisted until further notice from an impartial panel made up of myself, Bert Parks, and an eagle-eyed plastic surgeon. Since we own no pets, I am willing to waive the dog-poop provision. Do you think this will remove the romance from our marriage, dearest? If so, I could add a romance-preservation codicil to the general warmth-maintenance provision. How am I doing?

**Wanda:** Not at all well, Ralph, though only an elephant could miss your ponderously expressed point. I assume it's my turn.

**Ralph:** Don't hold back, sweetest. It may prove salvific for our connubial aspirations.

**Wanda:** All right. You will pick up your underwear four or more times each week or it will be confiscated and displayed for guests during dinner parties. You will remember the dates of my birthday and our anniversary or have them tattooed on your chest in mirror writing so you can meditate on them while shaving. We will go out to dinner at least once during October, even though it is the sacred time of the baseball play-offs, and you will remain eligible to talk in ten-second bursts or more during Monday-night football. You will cease all jokes about how I wake up in the middle of the night smelling dust, and you will learn how to operate the washing machine and the toaster.

**Ralph:** I think we have a meeting of the minds here, my pet. Can I add the provision that you won't say good-bye to everyone at parties, then stand in the doorway for an hour talking to the hostess, or is this common female behavior under genetic control?

**Wanda:** You're pushing it, Ralph. Does Sinatra really throw women through windows? Why don't they get a contract saying they can leave by the door like all the rest of the service people?

**Ralph:** That's ten bucks for two cracks about Frank, Wanda. By the way, dearest, does it seem dusty in here to you?

# BOYS
# WILL BE
# BOYS

# John
# Scanlon
# Meets
# St. Philomena

*This is a speech delivered at the surprise forty-seventh birthday party of John Scanlon, famous public relations man, wit, raconteur, ex-seminarian, and lifelong friend. Not all of this speech is true. Scanlon never accosted Jewish kids in The Bronx, though there was plenty of anti-Semitism in the area. He probably never even met Philomena. The name of his religious order is fictional, and was, in fact, thought up by a famous Catholic theologian and publisher, the late Frank Sheed.*

I think we all know the major achievements of John's career. How he was a New York City commissioner of economic planning during the exact years the city was going bankrupt. We know, too, his brilliant steps toward self-improvement, the famous breakfast with Paul Anka, the warmth lessons he took from John McEnroe, the inevitable comparisons with Margaret Trudeau.

But have we heard a single word tonight about the spiritual side of John Scanlon? No, we haven't. And yet it is crucial to understanding his success. Did you know, for instance, that the teenaged John Scanlon was devoted to street surveys on the subject of religion? Yes, while most of his peers were out acquiring hubcaps, John was doing the Lord's work, interviewing frail Jewish kids on the subject of religion. Though John was not conversant with modern sampling methods, he instinctively knew that these probes were more fruitful when conducted on the street, when the Jewish youth was confronted singly, and when there were seven or eight beefy Irish kids along to think up good questions.

Well, it was during this project—unfunded, by the way— that Scanlon came upon a most surprising finding: these frail Jewish youths were totally unable to account for their whereabouts during the crucifixion of Jesus. As you might expect, John acted firmly. More in sorrow than in anger, he announced that Jewish kids would not be allowed to march in the Bronx Holy Name Parade. And he put out his first press release, exonerating the Romans in Jesus' death. Just to be on the safe side, he also phoned apologies to Ruth Roman, Roman Polanski, and the bakers of Roman Meal bread.

Not long after, John took another decisive step in his quest for spirituality—he went into the seminary. Everyone knows Scanlon was a seminarian for several years, that's a matter of record. But he would have you believe that he joined the Irish Christian Brothers.

The Irish Christian Brothers are a famous order, with two highly developed skills: making brandy and hitting small boys with a heavy metal ruler exactly on the hip point. So naturally John would like to identify with that kind of success. But actually he never was an Irish Christian Brother at all. The truth is that he joined a less well-known religious order: the Little Brothers of the Dumb Ass of Jesus. Named, of course, for the silent (or dumb) donkey who was lucky enough to have that cribside seat at the birth of the baby Jesus.

According to Christian tradition, Jesus was born in the winter, and the warm breathing of the donkey helped keep mother and child alive during that perilous first night. Perhaps because of John's close identification with this tradition of silent service, even now whenever he enters a room, someone will call out fondly, "Here comes donkey breath."

Now, who are these Little Brothers and how do they fit in?

To answer that question I think I should explain that there is something of an intellectual hierarchy among the Catholic clergy. At the top are the Jesuits. All the brightest kids become Jesuits. Next come the Dominicans and the Basilians—they're smart, too—and the diocesan clergy, the regular parish priests who study bingo theory and get to run for monsignor, bishop, and pope. Lower down are a bunch of smaller orders, some good, some not. And near the bottom, sad to say, are the Little Brothers of the Dumb Ass of Jesus.

The Little Brothers do not, in truth, have rigorous entrance requirements. Either a pulse or a heartbeat will do, or failing either of those, a note from your mother. And so it was the one blustery day in the mid–nineteen fifties that John Scanlon showed up at the door of the Little Brothers, clutching a note from his mother.

Right away John cut to the heart of the matter by asking the brother who was working the door that day, "What do you have to do around here to get to be a saint?" The Little Brother scurried off without saying a word, and no one spoke to John for a year or two. This was the way of the Little Brothers. Then one day during the daily prayers to St. Tigris-Euphrates, virgin and martyr, Scanlon's question was answered. One of the older brothers whispered to him in chapel, "The name of the game here is humility, Brother John. To get to the top you're going to have to beat out some world-class humblers."

That was discouraging news, indeed, but John dedicated himself to humility, in his case, thoroughly justified humility. He even took up groveling. He groveled day and night. One day he said in despair, "I'll never get anywhere by groveling." Of course we here tonight, with the advantage of hindsight, can see that John was quite wrong. He was actually honing a basic skill.

But that's getting ahead of our story. John was deeply discouraged now—he felt he would never catch up to the wily veterans in the humility Olympics. The way to spiritual success seemed blocked.

Then one day an amazing thing happened. It was late at night. John had put in a hard day of free-style groveling, saying the rosary and taking cold showers. He had read the only reading material allowed in his cell—the little card warning each Little Brother against acquiring another Little Brother as "special friend." He had flipped his way through his holy card collection of virgin-martyrs, from #1 (St. Consumata, who, in

God's mercy, was saved from impending sexual assault by the fortunate intervention of a wild animal of some sort, which ate her) to #348 (St. Inundata, who had the presence of mind to drown herself in a waterfall in order to preserve her virginity and later, in a comeback, was named patron saint of unmarried car-wash attendants).

As I say, John was winding down for the night, unbuttoning his hair shirt—genuine beaver, and a gift from his parents, Gus and Mamie, who had acquired the garment on time from Fred the Furrier, then working the basement of Alexander's on Fordham Road. Actually Fred was not yet famous, and had not yet attracted the heroic epithet of "the Furrier." He was plain Fred Schwartz, just another local suspect in the slaying of Jesus.

Anyway, it was just as John was popping free the last beaver-clad button that the amazing incident occurred. There was a flash of brilliant light, a rustle of satin, and when John looked up, standing there right in his cell, in flagrant violation of the rules, was none other than St. Philomena, his favorite saint! As you can imagine, John fell to his knees, awestruck. His mouth was dry—he had never talked to a saint before. As a matter of fact, he had never talked to a woman before. He was Irish Catholic. John rubbed his eyes and the apparition spoke. "Schlep," she began—for Philomena was a worldly virgin-martyr and knew Yiddish cold. "Schlep," she explained once again. "Sainthood is not your schtick. Give it up, already."

I should explain here that Philomena, like everyone else, was not comfortable walking around like this, as if her hands were flippers. But that's the way she appeared in John's holy card set, #19, and she did want to be recognized on her rare personal appearances, so she stood like this. "Most beloved saint, known universally for your beatitude," Scanlon began— even then he knew enough to trowel it on thick—"beloved saint," said Scanlon, "I am called to the religious life, I just know I am."

"No, no Scanlon," replied the saint. "Look at you; hair on your shirt, hair on your palms, your skin shriveled to prunehood from all the cold showers. No you are not cut out for the pious life." It was at this point that the Great Saint spoke the words that altered the course of Scanlon's life: "You have a different and higher vocation. John Scanlon, you are called to a career in . . . MEDIA SCIENCE. I see you hobnobbing with big pols, pushing fancy foreign beers, explaining away folly at TV networks, and handling major motion pictures concocted by frail Jewish youths you used to interview in Highbridge. I would make up with them, bubbelah. Besides, the Romans did it. It was in the *Times.*"

Well, John was torn asunder by the most powerful emotions. Did he actually have it in him to be a media scientist? But how could he leave? For an instant he thought, is it possible to have it all—to be a Dumb Ass and a PR man? Well, once again, from our perspective, years later, we know the answer to that now familiar question, but to John it was new and perplexing. John was indeed powerfully drawn to media science, but he had a qualm.

Now, for those of you who do not know Jesuit casuistry, simplified of course for the Little Brothers, a qualm is weightier than a goad, but not as serious as a scruple. In fact, it works a bit like the table for apothecary weights: two goads to the qualm, three qualms to the scruple, four scruples to the pang, and two pangs to the doubt. Nobody in the Little Brothers had ever had a pang, much less a doubt, but qualms were permitted, so John had one of those.

"State your qualm," said Philomena.

"Well, Your Saintliness, I want to follow your lead, I truly do, but is it not true that media scientists sometimes . . . play loose with God's truth?"

The saint shook her head in holy disbelief. "Don't be a dumb ass, Little Brother," quipped Philomena, who, as I pointed out earlier, was quite worldly. "Scanlon, listen to me—I'm only going to say this once, so watch my lips: Truth is like a blazing light that bends and softens as it goes through a prism. John Scanlon, BE THAT PRISM."

Well, that did it. Scanlon's future was assured and Philomena disappeared. Scanlon spent a half hour searching the cell to see if she had dropped a glass slipper—his grasp of theology was never strong. But she left him something greater. That day he learned two important lessons: truth, like crude oil, is very valuable, but needs refining, and second, in the presence of a great person, it is always best to fall to your knees. And ever since, he has been a successful and qualm-free media scientist.

John, happy birthday.

# Boy George and Blue Doorknob Pride Day

**Ralph:** I have this great new idea for a rock group, Wanda. Four or five people come out onstage dressed as girls. Now, here's the twist: although decked out in female clothing, they really ARE girls. I know rock fans may be offended, but I want to stress that the group could do all the other rock-music things, like wearing pythons and Vermont flags, and naming their babies Futility and Wasserman Test. I wouldn't want to cut them off totally from their culture.

**Wanda:** I have the feeling that you are about to talk, in your usual measured tones, about the trend toward androgyny.

**Ralph:** If you insist, dearest. In the old days we had to make do with Alice Cooper, Mick Jagger, unisex barbers, and Renee

Richards, the tennis player who invented mixed singles. Now we are positively wealthy in sexual confusion. We have Michael Jackson, Annie Lennox, David Bowie, and a whole host of warbling transvestites like Boy George. Grace Jones was twice as ferocious as Wilt Chamberlain in *Conan the Destroyer,* at least for those who could tell them apart. Designers of uncertain sexuality are selling dresses to men and men's underwear to women. And any male actor who wants a Broadway role had better look good in a skirt. Travel writer Jan Morris (James Morris before the operation) wrote a spiffy piece in *Vanity Fair* pointing out that androgyny is a kind of mystic unification anticipated by the great French theologian Pierre Teilhard de Chardin. Talk about harmonic convergence. Of course, Teilhard, being dead, is unavailable for rebuttal. It makes a guy like me, still struck in a single gender, feel like he just can't make it on the cutting edge of the culture.

**Wanda:** You were never a serious threat to do much edge-cutting, Ralph. I really don't think you have to grow red-faced about all this. The Republic won't fall if Madonna puts on a pair of Jockey shorts and Boy George remains unjailed for wearing lipstick.

**Ralph:** Gosh, isn't that what Lesley Stahl was getting at in her landmark *Face the Nation* program on androgyny? Just imagine: the nation was faced with Boy George, Jerry Falwell, John Naisbitt, and Gore Vidal, all on the same show! Naisbitt is the author of *Megatrends,* and he thinks androgyny is the eleventh American megatrend. He's got them all numbered, like Nixon's crises. Boy George said his fame is making the world safe for cross-dressers everywhere. Falwell said he thought boys were boys and girls were girls, but then he's always been controversial. Vidal said macho guys are starting to wear skirts because they're bored and have no outlet for their macho skills. Maybe old Gore could mingle a bit more with some unemployed steelworkers and raise his skirt issue with them. You have to admire his lonely fight against coherence. Anyhow, Lesley is a terrific journalist, and I feel confident she'll bounce back from this.

**Wanda:** The show wasn't as dopey as you say, hardhearted one. Naisbitt thinks men are adopting more "feminine" characteristics like sensitivity, and women more "masculine" ones like aggressiveness. What's wrong with that? He said he thought the readjustment of sexual roles was "probably the most important thing that's going on in this century in America." Jan Morris believes the sexes are becoming recognizably more alike, "converging upon some physical median." She thinks sex will die out in a couple of thousand years, and writes in *Vanity Fair* that "perhaps we are all on the road to intersex; perhaps the world of today, by some inexplicable perceptions, sees characters like Boy George and me as examples of its own sexual future."

**Ralph:** Cogently argued, light of my life. Suddenly I share your piercing insight: in the future we will all be boys with strawberry lipstick and travel writers who have had their parts removed. Why didn't I see this before? And we shall all copulate like plants, sending little runners out along the ground to create pea pods full of even more befuddled young sprouts, who in turn will produce their own tiny vegetables. The world shall be a truck farm, dearest.

**Wanda:** In the future, we won't need the Tarzan-Jane relationships, and whether you are male or female won't matter. The appeal of cross-dressing and sexually ambivalent rock stars is that they tease people like you, with rigid ideas about sex roles, and prepare the way for more relaxed attitudes.

**Ralph:** I am definitely trying to relax, Wanda. As a matter of fact, I want to go on record as backing the inalienable right of adolescent guitar-bangers everywhere to try on Mommy's clothes. It is the sacred duty of every rock star to irritate as many American parents as possible, and they were coping with this thankless task quite nicely until all the megatrendy analysts had to butt in and declare the dress-up game meaningful. What you have to conclude is that it's extremely hard to be a wacko in America these days. Paint yourself blue and call yourself a doorknob, and nobody titters or sends for help. They adopt you. Phil Donahue invites you over for a deeply empathic discussion. Jan Morris sees you as a telegram from the year 4000. Someone will start a Blue Doorknob Pride Day and swinging psychiatrists will announce that there's a little bit of blue doorknob in all of us, if only we had the courage to let it out. America's a great country, Wanda. Everybody in it is normal.

**Wanda:** Ralph, do you ever get the feeling you're ranting? Not out of control, of course, but just sort of carrying on?

**Ralph:** Wanda, I think you just got in touch with your tough masculine side! As your husband, I find my own feminine side bubbling up androgynously. Can I try on some of your things? Be a good fellow and let me wear that darling blue number with the pleats. . . . Wanda, what's happening? Are you angry about something? . . . Maybe we should talk.

# Exclusive:
# Ronald Reagan's
# Memoirs!

**M**y editor, who is smart about such matters, says I have to explain this joke. Okay. President Reagan, a likable fellow and a
pleasure to watch, was nobody's idea of a master of detail. One of
his minor flaws was the occasional tendency to confuse the movies
with real life. Several times he gave moving speeches about an
unnamed winner of the Congressional Medal of Honor, quoting
the hero's last words just before his plane crashed into the English
Channel. This raised two important questions about the hero: was
he the Dana Andrews character in Wing and a Prayer, and if he
wasn't, how did the President know his last words?

Well, I read where the Kremlin gave its highest award one day
to a Spanish interpreter living in Moscow. This puzzled me.

Why a gold medal to an interpreter, a man who had lived quietly in such Spanish-speaking countries as Spain, Cuba, and Mexico? Life in those countries may be difficult, but surely not everyone who lives there deserves a medal. So why the honor? Well, a journalist who knows more about the facts than I do discovered that the interpreter had spent twenty-three years in a Mexican jail. Digging further into the story, the journalist learned that this interpreter was the very man who had buried the mountaineer's ice axe in the head of Leon Trotsky. Moscow gave him his gold medal for murder.

Now, that set me thinking, something I like to do now and then if I have time. My memory went back to one thrilling story of American heroism during the war. A B-17 coming back from a raid over the Channel was so badly shot up that the commander ordered everyone to bail out. The crew jumped. The commander took one last look around the plane to make sure everyone had gone, and to his surprise, he noticed a young ball-turret gunner pinned in the wreckage, so badly wounded that he could not get up. The boy, understandably, cried out in terror, because the plane was heading into the sea, but the commander took his hand and said, "Never mind, son, we'll ride it down together." Congressional Medal of Honor, posthumously awarded.

Now, there are two points I'd like to make about this story. One, of course, is that we give medals to self-sacrificing heroes, and they give them to axe-murderers, an important and little-noticed difference between our two forms of government. The bedrock of our strength is our moral and spiritual character; theirs is the willingness to split heads in Mexico. Also, if they give gold medals for murder, maybe it's just as well that we boycotted the 1980 Moscow Olympics.

My second point is this. The story about the commander is a real-life story. It really happened. Some among us, giving way to cynicism, say, "Mr. President, how can we possibly know what the commander said, when he and the injured gunner both died in the crash, and therefore were in no position to be interviewed?" Well, there's probably a very simple answer to that. Maybe the last jumper, perhaps only fifty feet or so below the plane at the time, heard the commander's voice on the way down. More likely the commander got on the radio in the seconds before the crash, and passed on his last stirring words to the American people, via the BBC. Or it could be that the wounded gunner wrote down the words, folded them in an asbestos wallet, and attached them to a fireproof weather balloon so that this emotional comment could someday be used in a presidential address.

I don't really know the facts. That is not my specialty. But I know that the incident did not come from a movie. Sure, a movie of the incident was later produced, with Dana Andrews speaking those very moving words. But remember, that movie was made in black and white, and I have a strong recollection of a colorized exchange between the two valiant airmen. After all, I could not have confused a movie with real life. Besides, no one doubts that Trotsky was really axed by the Communist assassin. Why do they doubt only stories of American heroes? This reminds me of another stirring tale of American valor, this one occurring, I believe, during the Revolutionary War. Nathan Hale, I think it was, was about to be hanged as a spy. His British captor said something like "It looks like curtains for you, Nathan," and the great patriot replied coolly, "Frankly, my dear, I don't give a damn." What presence of mind. Now, I don't have to remind you that there are no stories like this about the Russian Revolution, and I'll tell you why. Our system celebrates moral and spiritual character. It is the highest aspiration of our people, bred in the bone of every American. Let us hope and pray that there will always be brave Americans unwilling to give a damn, but perfectly willing to ride this one down together.

# Stop the
# Press–Men
# Have Feelings Too

Long Beach, Ca. (AP)—Capping a ten-year, multimillion-dollar state-financed effort, a hard-nosed microchip executive today became the first man in California to get in touch with his feelings.

The startling feat, watched by enthralled millions on television, was immediately hailed by former governor Jerry Brown as "an historic milestone in our exploration into inner space."

"What a ride!" exclaimed Bruce Babble, 32, emerging from his tiny, windowless capsule at 11:32 A.M. today, ending a risky and grueling six-minute experiment in which he was intentionally exposed to unspecified but volatile emotional material.

His face wreathed in a broad smile, the weary Babble

quipped "I'm A-OK. Hey, I'm up front and centered and I've touched some really deep chords." A-OK is inner-space jargon for "Affect Okay." The meaning of these phrases uttered by Babble was not immediately apparent. Some scientists believe they are essentially meaningless words triggered by randomly firing brain neurons under extraordinary stress.

A team of medical experts reported later that Babble was "supernormal," with a heartbeat, blood count, and IQ level all unchanged. Aside from slight nausea and a brief bout of vomiting, so far he has displayed none of the distressing side effects which scientists believed would accompany any male attempt to feel actual emotions, among them a much higher speaking voice and the disappearance of facial hair.

### CREDIT TO HIS SEX

Proud Californians from Yorba Linda to Eureka exulted in the stunning achievement. "He made it, he made it," exclaimed a tearful Sausalito matron, Marge Metcalf, 54. "It was horrible listening to that countdown, not knowing what would happen. He risked everything, didn't he? He's a hero and a credit to his sex."

"He did it for all of us," gulped Gus Grizzle of Bodega Bay during a break in all-star wrestling. "Only he knows why." Tina Taylor, 23, a Sacramento hairstylist, was politely enthusiastic. "This kind of thing is quite a small step for womankind," she said, "but it's definitely a giant step forward for mankind."

Many women suggested that Babble's experiment may point the way toward a new type of relationship, marked by two-way communication between the sexes. "Two people feeling in one household," cried Sally Tompkins of Pebble Beach.

"What a concept!" Yet many women around the state called for caution. "Men having feelings is theoretically possible, of course," conceded feminist theoretician Esmerelda Apgar, "but let's not jump to conclusions. We have to go over the data very carefully."

Babble's journey into his own psyche appears to settle a question that has plagued social scientists for years: Could a human male, adapted so perfectly for life without sentiment of any kind, actually locate and get in touch with his own hypothetical feelings?

### WITH EYES TAPED OPEN

"Never before has a male human being been asked for an emotional response other than anger or boredom," said thrice-married Wanda Firtle of Laguna Beach. In fact, several churchmen and other moralists have raised a question about the propriety of subjecting a normal male to such pressures. (A storm of ethical protests arose last month after a controversial experiment at the State Feeling Center, located in a heart-shaped building on the campus of the University of California at Santa Cruz. In the test, an admittedly rugged male was told he would be shown *Monday Night Football,* but was actually locked into a room with his eyes taped open in front of a made-for-TV movie about a lonely dietician's last chance for love.)

A spokesperson for the California Inner Space Program (CISP) revealed that Babble located his feelings quickly, and experienced stress only when CISP leaders asked him to hold on to one feeling for a full four minutes. During this period, which the spokesperson described as "a rocky ride . . . truly harrowing," Babble suffered disorientation, and briefly groped toward the escape hatch.

Unlike the chimp used in last year's experiment, Babble was at the controls of his capsule, able to touch various dials and levers which correct for panic, irony, distancing, subject-changing humor, previous engagements, sports reveries, and other indicators of male stress.

As launch time approached, rehearsals were staged using actual feelings under realistic conditions in a centrifuge in Santa Barbara. The experimental feelings, borrowed from women and carefully stored under antiseptic conditions, are said to have included sadness, joy, surprise, and empathy.

Although no announcement has been made about which of these feelings were used in the televised experiment, a source inside CISP said that the agency was afraid to expose Babble to more than seven seconds of empathy, for fear of risking permanent damage.

### ALWAYS A GOOD KID

Instead, CISP strategists are said to have spent most of the time exposing Babble to higher and higher doses of sadness. "We have reason to believe that all the best women will soon be looking around for men capable of crying," said a highly placed source. "Babble is a bachelor, and after all he has been through, the least we can do is give him an edge he can use."

Babble's normality was established two months ago in a standard psychological test for males: while viewing pictures of mangled accident victims, his face showed no response at all. "He was always a good kid," said his mother, Twyla Babble.

# Firebelles
# in the
# Night

**Wanda:** Ralph, what do you think of women fire fighters?

**Ralph:** Not much, my sweet. It's a bit like using partially blind people as umpires.

**Wanda:** Why did I ask?

**Ralph:** Perhaps to depict me as a sputtering sexist, my own true love. Alas, your unvoiced criticism is wide of the mark. Even Phil Donahue knows that the best women can't compete with the best men in feats of strength and stamina. Upper-body strength, you know. This may be why there are so few women in pro football. I don't see why standards should be any lower in pro fire fighting.

**Wanda:** Right, Ralph. All the fire fighters just have to be male, just like all the doctors, lawyers, and alchemists were male when you were growing up in the ninth century.

**Ralph:** I didn't invent biology, dear love, and as far as I know, none of my friends did either. Who do you want dragging you out of a fire, a brute or a firelady with correct feminist principles?

**Wanda:** Anybody who can pass a fair test. Why do you think Atlanta, San Diego, Seattle, and a dozen or so other cities have hired women for their fire departments?

**Ralph:** Normal pressure-group politics. Once all the lobbies win their nonnegotiable demands, your local fire department will probably have three women, one creationist, a couple of low-impact aerobics teachers, a handicapped swami, a deprogrammed Moonie, and one fully self-actualized bisexual vegetarian. The town will burn down, but what the hell, that's a small price to pay for a truly trendy fire department.

**Wanda:** Ralph, the veins are standing out in your neck. Look, women don't want quotas or special preferences, just a fair shot at the jobs. It's not written in stone that only men can extinguish flames.

**Ralph:** That sounds good, but it doesn't work out that way. Look at what happened in New York. The city had thirteen thousand males and no females in its fire department. So the women said, "Just give us a fair chance at passing the test." Eighty women took the physical test, and—guess what—all eighty failed. Did the women say, "Gee it takes more strength than I thought to be a fireman?" No, of course not. They decided the test was sexist; they sued. And they won.

**Wanda:** Hold on, Ralph. There were real problems with the city test. In the handgrip test, nobody told the women that you could adjust the machine for smaller hand size. They couldn't get leverage, and they all did poorly. A candidate is supposed to run the mile in four minutes fifty seconds. What's that got to do with being a good fire fighter? And the part where you have to carry a hundred-twenty-pound dummy up a flight of stairs—the dummy was canvas-covered and cylindrical, so people with shorter arms couldn't quite grasp it right. How often do you have to plunge into a burning building to rescue a slippery cylinder? Some of these tests are dopey, and the rest are created by and for males.

**Ralph:** You mean the tests were created by pros, and now they'll be adjusted by and for amateurs. I hope they don't invent a test for women eye surgeons that a high-school graduate can pass after a week of home study.

**Wanda:** Ralph, I'm not wild about your analogies.

**Ralph:** They're not wild, Wanda dearest. The goodhearted federal judge in the New York City case made one of those stupefying rulings. The city was to hire forty-five women as fire fighters—and the department was ordered to devise a test women could pass. Terrific. That's how we ruined our schools, by designing trick tests that anybody with a heartbeat could pass. This is worse—lives are at stake here. With all due respect to the judiciary, I think the judge has a goodly portion of pudding between his ears. You could use the same logic to force the NBA to lower its baskets five feet and accept a quota of dwarfs. By the way, there was talk that those forty-five women the city has to hire could get forty thousand dollars on their first working day—imaginary back pay for the time they would have worked if they could have passed the test. *Alice in Wonderland* stuff, Wanda.

**Wanda:** Calm yourself, Ralph. I'm not going to bother reasoning with you about how good women might be if they were offered the kind of training programs, support, and encouragement that men get routinely. Anyway, did you really think, after all these years of feminism, that fire fighting was going to be left blissfully alone as an all-male profession? There are only a few hundred women on the job now, but in a few years it will be thousands, so get used to the idea.

**Ralph:** I'm used to the idea right now. From now on, all the fires in this house will be on the first floor, right near the door, where even a court-appointed woman can put them out. And if I'm ever trapped under a beam or something, I'll nod knowingly if a firelady stops by and says, "Sorry, I can't lift a hundred twenty pounds. The judge said that I could save three forty-pound people instead."

**Wanda:** Just look at Nancy Sweeney, who jogged, lifted weights, did push-ups, and carried her kids up and down three flights of stairs to get in shape. She not only passed the Indianapolis fire department test, she was named Rookie of the Year. Betsy Powell, a paramedic in the Dallas fire department, could also pull you out from under a beam, where maybe you belong. She admits that men in the department have greater upper-body strength, but she's learned to compensate by using her legs more in lifting. She's in great shape, she's served as engine foreman, and her captain says she is "exceptionally good" at what she does. He says she's not strong enough to pull down a shiplap ceiling, whatever that is, so he has someone else do that. Big deal. There are always some people in every department who can't do certain things, the older guys, for instance. But they are all valuable, so will you please shut up.

**Ralph:** Well, if the women take orders, and stay out of the way, maybe each department could carry a decorative firelady or two without messing up.

**Wanda:** Even if they are slippery and cylindrical. Say goodnight, Ralph.

# Beasts
# of the
# City

**B**y all accounts, Albert Vidal, A Spanish mime who performs at zoos around the world, was a smash hit when he brought his act to Miami. Taking up residence for three days among the Galápagos tortoises in an outdoor pen at the Metro Zoo, Vidal unfurled his impression of urban man, watching television, poring over *Advertising Age*, and sleeping in striped pajamas on a platform bed, all for a fee of $10,000.

Zoogoers howled in recognition as Vidal brushed his teeth, chatted on the phone, and spent thirty minutes elaborately stripping and eating a banana. "It's the same as seeing a camel or any other species in the zoo," said the mime, shrugging off his triumph. During his performance, Vidal remained silent, as mimes are apt to do, but he shook hands with onlookers and allowed them to feed him candy. In one bravura touch, he sprayed the open air with wintergreen room freshener.

In many respects, of course, Vidal succeeded admirably in evoking urban man. His skill at lounging around inescapably brings to mind the work habits of certain urban unions. And going about one's business with a crowd of strangers looking on certainly goes to the heart of the urban experience. But there were sorry flaws as well. Does any reader of *Ad Age* really wear polyester? What urban man has thirty minutes to devote to the consumption of a single banana? And what kind of urban experience omits all reference to discos, purse snatchers, joggers, yogurt sauces, fashion designers, and the myriad other problems afflicting city life?

Clearly the Metro Zoo erred in installing a single urban animal instead of a full bestiary. The next time around the zookeepers should shop for some of the following types, all available for under $10,000:

**Blasterman.** In an age notable for selfishness blasterman is one urban type dedicated to sharing. Day and night he shoulders the heavy burden of an enormous radio or recorder and shares its compelling music with delighted listeners for several blocks in every direction. Surveys show that blasterman justifiably looks down on Walkman, another strolling and tuneful urbanite, but one who unaccountably declines to share his or her musical merriment.

**PBSman.** This familiar urban specimen is readily identified by his corduroy jacket and cloth bag, emblazoned with the emblem of his local public television channel. He enlivens many a wine-and-cheese party with pertinent observations on secondhand smoke and the Heimlich maneuver, and he is especially jubilant each October when the Nobel Prize for literature is awarded to yet another Samoan poet or Andean shepherd.

**Powerman.** A businessman with a power haircut and power suit who acts powerfully toward all comers except the maître d', who grants him a power table in a power restaurant. Powerman's guide to life is Michael Korda, who recommends practicing one's power gaze, presumably in front of a power mirror.

**Lightman/Liteman.** The antithesis of powerman. Liteman drinks lite wine, listens to lite music, and frequently sets up light housekeeping with one of the sexes, keeping matters light.

**Jogman.** Known by his or her expansive sense of well-being, which is apparently derived from the wearing of zany clothing and from a tireless commitment to knee and foot damage. Somewhat like trees, jogman improves urban life for the rest of us by inhaling great quantities of auto exhaust fumes from the atmosphere. Anthropologists are frankly confused about the motivation of jogman. Some say it is the desire to avoid a heart attack, while others insist it is the desire to achieve one.

**Touristman.** Garbed in the authentic polyester favored by Vidal, T-man travels to the city via an $89 flight and a $300 cab ride from the airport. Risking sunburn of the throat while marveling at the tall buildings, he will purchase an I-HEART-THE-CITY T-shirt and an original cast record of *Beatlemania* (not a real performance by Beatle imitators, but an incredible simulation.)

**Therapyman.** Years on the couch have yielded many piercing moment of self-revelation to therapyman, among them the insight that he is much too hard on himself and is not on earth to live up to other people's expectations. Therapyman is in constant contact with his feelings, an absorbing activity that leaves little time to get in touch with the feelings of anybody else.

**Workwoman.** She goes to work wearing ruffles at the neck and a tailored jacket (indicating a lack of daytime sexuality), plus dark panty hose and large scuffed sneakers, faintly suggesting Minnie Mouse plodding off to the office after a creative divorce from Mickey. Workwoman is part of the historical shift from the home, which is now minus 100,000 people to watch the kids, to the law office, which features an equal number of surplus and totally unnecessary lawyers.

**Androgynous Person.** Forsaking *male* and *female* as outmoded categories, the modern androgene is a striking transient on the urban scene, importantly influenced by guess-my-sex rock stars and sexually variant designers. To achieve the proper effect, males learn to flounce and cry a good deal, while women must attain male levels of pointless aggression. The androgene is so indecisively dressed that the only way to tell male from female, according to informed scientists, is to scrutinize these rare specimens in a domestic setting: the male is the one who refuses to help out around the house.

**Trendyman.** Trendy is found at all the right discos and beaneries, frequently taking nourishment nasally and wearing clothes too garish even for jogman. Something has gone radically wrong with trendyman's diet recently. He has astonished his keepers by refusing sushi and pesto and demanding fiddlehead ferns and Moussy.

**Developerman.** Responding to new concern about exposure to the sun and skin cancer, developer tosses up so many high-rise monstrosities that cities will never again be plagued by sunlight.

**Gentrified Man.** This is a working man who has recently learned that his $60-a-month semislum apartment is about to be converted into a $600,000 coop or a nighttime playpen for vibrant yuppies. The shock is frequently assuaged by the news that this is merely the free market at work, and that he is, after all, eligible for the insider's $500,000 price on his old flat.

Because of cross-breeding and gene-splicing, colorful new variations of these urban species are appearing all the time. Vidal's gentle mime does not seem ready for life among these specimens. His thick-shelled roommates are in far better shape. Galápagos tortoises are true survivors.

# TOUCHY, TOUCHY

# The Stewardi Aren't Smiling Anymore

**Wanda:** How was your flight in from the Coast, dear?

**Ralph:** Perfectly adequate, my pet. But something must have been bothering all the stewardi. None of them seemed able to smile much.

**Wanda:** You are missing yet another social trend, Ralph. A lot of them have decided to cut back on full-time professional happiness. Lawyers and accountants don't have to smile relentlessly for hours at a stretch. Why should flight attendants?

**Ralph:** Let me get my coat off, dearest. I want to brace myself on the off chance that someone I love intends to launch a hearty feminist harangue. Am I about to hear that smiling is bad for women?

**Wanda:** Right you are, Ralph. In her book *The Managed Heart,* Arlie Russell Hochschild says that the perpetually frozen smile of flight attendants is a classic bit of commercial manipulation that propels many of them into minibreakdowns. One flight attendant calls it "artificially created elation," the sort of thing that turns women into ticket-selling objects, not to mention flying bunnies.

**Ralph:** Let us lapse briefly into logic, dearest. The average flight contains 70 to 80 people who are totally convinced that the plane is going to crash, maybe 50 who are enraged by the mandatory 30-minute delay in getting off the ground, and another 100 or so who are busy getting giddy or truculent through the magic of booze. Under the circumstances, which is better: a calming smile or a conventionally irritating dose of tooth-grinding feminism?

**Wanda:** Pilots don't have to chuckle when they give one of those breezy Chuck Yeager speeches saying that there's nothing to worry about even though the plane has no landing wheels. Females are assigned the social role of grinning all the time, Ralph. It's one way men keep women in their place. Vivian Gornick talks about "that damned dazzling smile," and Nancy Henley, a social psychologist, calls it "woman's badge of appeasement" that placates the more powerful male. Henley did some experiments showing that women smile 89 percent of the time in social encounters, while men smile only 67 percent. And 26 percent more of female-to-male smiles are not returned.

**Ralph:** The idea of all those women's smiles dying unrequited is nauseating, dearest. We've got to get men beaming at full throttle to close the smile gap.

**Wanda:** Don't start, Ralph. Even some of you men are beginning to get the hang of this. Erving Goffman, the expert in nonverbal communication, once wrote that women are almost always shown smiling in ads to show their deference to men. When there's a smiling man in an ad, the woman usually has to smile twice as broadly to indicate her subordinate status. Then there's the book *Winning Moves: The Body Language of Selling.* It warns women sales representatives not to smile too much or too early when calling on a prospect. Ken Delmar, the businessman who wrote the book, says, "Most men are quite ready not to take you seriously. Don't give them any ammunition." A woman who smiles too much is pigeonholed as frivolous, Ralph.

**Ralph:** These are certainly deep waters, Wanda. As your local representative of the uptrodden gender, I frankly had no idea that cheerfulness was a patriarchal plot. If I correctly recall our last forty-two arguments, you have been telling me that men not only have trouble expressing their feelings, they may even be emotionally tone deaf. Wouldn't it be logical for you to argue that women smile more because they are less blocked emotionally, not because niceness is a symbol of servitude?

**Wanda:** Nice try, my cunning hubby. In fact, the smile is a hostility deflector. It's trotted out more often by disadvantaged groups because they are afraid of the power of the majority. Women smile more than men because they have to appease men and because everyone assumes we are responsible for the emotional tone of social life.

**Ralph:** *Au contraire,* my ideological one. A bunch of psychological studies show that you can improve your own mood by smiling. Since when is that wrong for women? The smile is also a famed instrument of social bonding, and females are simply better at it than males. I would say that women's greater tendency to smile is built in by evolution, probably as a tool to make them respond quicker and better to infants. Umpteen studies show that little girls are organized to respond better to people than little boys. They are more sensitive to the crying of other infants, and even in the first two or three days of life they spend much more time smiling than newborn boys do. Doubtless this is an early prefeminist attempt to placate the patriarchy.

**Wanda:** Those are biologically based smiles, Ralph, and they have nothing to do with the beaming bimbo that you men have created as a model for all women. The pasted-on smile that we are supposed to wear marks us as sexy little numbers, perpetually featherheaded and reassuring to men.

**Ralph:** Be of good cheer, Wanda. Your doting husband understands and accepts your ideological commitment to facial unpleasantness. But surely even a rampaging feminist needn't be a sourpuss in the privacy of her own home. Now how about a nice industrial-strength smile for your doting husband? If you wish, we can pull down all the shades first. And I can assure you that the Bureau of Feminist Rectitude will never hear about it from me. Come on, Wanda, get those corners up.

**Wanda:** Ralph, the only difference between you and a leering construction worker is that your request for a smile is not accompanied by a full repertoire of smacking and sucking noises. Also, the average construction worker is probably lots more sensitive.

**Ralph:** Smile and the world smiles with you, Wanda. As I believe Shulamith Firestone once observed, "You can catch more flies with honey—"

**Wanda:** Not one more word, Ralph!

**Ralph:** "—than you can with feminist theory." Good night, dearest.

# Why All
# Villains Are
# Thin, Middle-Aged
# WASPS

**W**endy's classic "Where's the Beef?" commercial was a small masterpiece of lunacy and perfect timing. But the Michigan Commission on Services to the Aging was not amused. The hamburger drama, said commission chairman Joseph Rightley, gave the impression that "elderly people, in particular women, are senile, deaf, and have difficulty seeing." The point of the ad, of course, was that non-Wendy's hamburgers are so small that anyone would have difficulty seeing them, regardless of race, creed, sex, age, or membership in an organized pressure group.

To their credit, the Gray Panthers issued a statement declaring Wendy's innocent of ageism and pronouncing themselves pleased that the three women were not shown as quiet victims in the face of clear hamburger abuse. The Panthers, as it happens, have their own problems with overreaction, attacking the immortal Christmas song "Grandma Got Run Over by a Reindeer" (Grandma had too much eggnog and forgot her pills) and letting scriptwriters know that old people should not be shown with wheelchairs, canes, or hearing aids. In supporting Wendy's, the Panthers took the opportunity to fire a warning shot disguised as a compliment: "It is especially accurate to portray the elderly as the critical and discriminating consumers they are, from hamburgers to health care." One may wonder why it is "especially accurate" to portray oldsters as all-around shrewd consumers when the rest of us are bilked regularly enough and will presumably remain just as bilkable in our sunset years.

The choice of language by the Panthers and Mr. Rightley gives the game away. In an age of organized touchiness, the goal of lobbying groups is not to erase stereotypes but to reverse them so that there is never an image of any group that falls very far short of idealization. Infirm oldsters and ethnic criminals exist in the real world but they are not to exist on TV or in the movies.

Stage and screen these days are littered with the gored oxen of one outraged group or another. Puerto Ricans and blacks sued to block the filming of *Fort Apache, The Bronx*, declaring it racist. Homosexuals tried to disrupt production of *Cruising*. Oriental activists protested a recent Charlie Chan movie, forcing the maker of the film into a preproduction whine about his abiding respect for the famous Chinese sleuth. Sioux Indians demonstrated against the book *Hanta Yo*, which contained passages on the ferocity of the Sioux. Under the guidance of many Sioux advisors, the television version toned down the savagery and concentrated on the spiritual side of the tribe.

The feminist group Women Against Pornography zapped a Hanes hosiery commercial as sexist, which surprised the ad agency involved. Men were indeed looking at a woman's legs, as they tend to do in "Gentlemen Prefer Hanes" commercials, but the story line of the ad was a female's successful attempt to join an all-male club over the stuffy objections of a Colonel Blimp type. In Congress, Mario Biaggi demanded hearings on the issue of whether two productions of *Rigoletto* were offensive to Italian-Americans. Both the English National Opera and the Virginia Opera updated Verdi's tale of a contract killing from sixteenth century Mantua to twentieth century New York City. Amid charges of "stereotyping," the opera executives backed down a bit: the Metropolitan Opera (host to the English company) dropped all references to the Mafia and Cosa Nostra, and the Virginia Opera inserted a program note apologizing for its bullet-marked poster. Cubans and Cuban-Americans were officially affronted by the Al Pacino version of *Scarface.* Producer Martin Bregman, who is Jewish, felt compelled to point out that the film shows more crooked Jews than crooked Cubans. A Miami city commissioner helpfully suggested that criticism could be avoided by making the protagonist an agent of Fidel Castro, sent to Florida to discredit Cuban-Americans.

Even generic criminals with all-purpose names like Miller and Greene can raise a hackle or two, at least if they appear in westerns: some members of the National Association for Outlaw and Lawman History argue that the lawmen were not as good or the outlaws as bad as presented in the movies and on TV. Given the number of watchful pressure groups, it would seem the path of wisdom for filmmakers to make their villains middle-aged, middle-sized heterosexual Anglo males. But even this is risky. Social scientists Linda and Robert Lichter complain that prime-time television criminals are usually "middle- or upper-class white males over age thirty" and more apt to be rich than poor. The Lichters were acting as hired guns for the Media Institute, a conservative pro-business lobby. The institute, along with the Mobil Oil Corporation and Accuracy in Media, would like to purge the tube of dishonest businessmen.

The lobby for disabled people has been particularly vociferous, and occasionally implacable. For the film *Voices,* a love story about a deaf woman and a would-be rock singer, MGM hired deaf actors and a deaf professor as a technical adviser. This proved insufficient to placate the deafness lobby, which boycotted the film because it lacked captions and because the heroine was played by Amy Irving, who can hear. MGM plaintively said it had gone "to all ends" to find a deaf actress for the lead, and wondered why it was being punished for producing a positive film about deaf people. Even a later version with captions added failed to satisfy the lobbyists. Jerry Lewis may be under the impression that he is doing good work with his muscular dystrophy telethon, but he has been under fire for years from various disabled groups for featuring helpless children rather than self-sufficient adults, for inducing pity and for implying that the disabled cannot make it without outside help. Presumably the only surefire way to raise money for the needy is to demonstrate that the recipients don't actually need it.

Much of the yelping at the media seems deeply trivial. A New York coven of witches complained when ABC reran *Rosemary's Baby.* A marine biologist was bothered by the negative image of sharks in *Jaws*, and UFO enthusiasts groused when a woman was raped by an alien from outer space on *Fernwood 2 Night*. Their point was that space aliens don't go around raping people, and indeed there is little evidence that they do. The National Association to Aid Fat Americans mounted a stout protest against the Dom DeLuise movie *Fatso*. The group does not mind the word *fat*, but *fatso* is a red flag. NAAFA also took a swipe at the Diet Pepsi campaign for showing "emaciated, almost anorectic women." No rebuttal has been recorded, possibly because there is as yet no thin people's lobby to return the fire.

What would life have been like in Hollywood if there had been a short people's lobby or a Hibernian Anti-Defamation League when Jimmy Cagney was shooting up the back lot at Warner's? Or when the first Dracula movies were made? ("Neck sucking is another way of loving"—Vampire Liberation.) Though the past is hazy, the future is not. Here is how a few old-time classics will be remade to deflect all criticism:

*Tom Sawyer*. Indian Joseph, a deaf brain surgeon and weekend spelunker, is falsely accused of hanky-panky with noted feminist attorney Becky Thatcher in the caves above Hannibal, Mo., an All-American city. Once cleared, Joseph and Thatcher team up with the Junior Chamber of Commerce to defend Tom Sawyer, a young entrepreneur defamed by antibusiness townspeople for practicing capitalism with his employee and fence painter Huck Finn. Prejudice against women, businessmen, Indians, and deaf people is delightfully exploded.

*The Public Enemy's Kiss of Death*. A mentally alert lady in a wheelchair, fresh from an early finish in the Boston Marathon, shoves Richard Widmark down a flight of stairs in justified retribution for centuries of male oppression. For much the same reason, Mae Clark grinds half a grapefruit in the face of tall but sexist breakfast partner James Cagney. Though clad in a nightie, Ms. Clark is shown carrying barbells and a briefcase to indicate that she is a serious person, not a sexual object. ("At last, a movie about strong achieving women!"—Alan Alda. "Thanks for exploding the myth about stairway safety"—Otis Elevator Company. "We resent the stereotyped connection between grapefruit and violence. Legal threat to follow."—Florida Citrus Commission.)

*Mr. Dante's Inferno.* Dante and Virgil tour the underworld, which contains no one of Italian extraction and, in fact, no one of any ethnicity at all. They are shocked to find, however, that many sexual eclectics, venture capitalists, smokers, and members of other disadvantaged minorities are being cruelly punished for their alternative life-styles. "This is right out of the Middle Ages," quips Dante. Virgil is quick to point out that many short people, left-handers, and riders of stationary bicycles are among the tormented, thus invoking tired stereotypes. A clever ACLU lawyer closes the place on a building-code violation. Said the attorney: "It was just hell."

*Moby Dick.* Captain Ahab, an emotionally well-adjusted and two-legged maritime naturalist, pursues a generic gray whale with binoculars and a Peterson field guide. ("If this be 'obsession,' let's have more of it!"—Save the Whales. "Call us happy. Can't wait for Moby II"—International Union of Seafarers.)

*The Lone Ranger.* Crusading reporter and leading gay activist Bruce ("Tonto") Redmann goes under cover to unmask a deranged and excessively macho former lawman turned vigilante. Best scene: removal of the mask, representing the inauthentic and alienated self. Mr. Ranger is depicted as far from typical of most former lawmen, most heterosexuals, and most white folks in general. His derangement is sensitively handled and shown to be the result of societal prejudice and a mistaken reading of the Miranda decision. All those perforated by Mr. Ranger's silver bullets are likewise portrayed sympathetically, and Tonto bans the use of the word *outlaw* as stigmatizing. ("A tale we can all identify with"—Native American Gays [NAG]. "Okay with us"—Society of North American Retired Lawmen [SNARL]. "Shows we are all victims"—Ollie North [ON]).

*The Back of Notre Dame.* Handsome college football star F. X. Quasimodo, vacationing in France, saves a perfectly self-sufficient but bound-and-gagged professional woman from a fiery death at the hands of a maddened Parisian throng. The movie deftly makes the much needed social statement that people supposedly "handicapped" by lower back pain can easily perform impressive feats of rope-swinging and feminist-lifting. ("A bell-ringer!"—the Reverend Theodore Hesburgh. "The first positive film about a man whose name ends in a vowel"— Carmine "the Snake" Persico. "Kudos for a great flick about Frogtown"—the Reverend Jesse Jackson.)

# Ophelia the Carnophobe

**Ralph:** Ophelia, have some meat.

**Ophelia:** I don't eat corpses anymore, Dad. It's gross.

**Ralph:** Say what?

**Wanda:** Try to shun apoplexy when you hear this, Ralph— Ophelia has become a vegetarian.

**Ralph:** Hand me the phone, Wanda. We can get her some help. No matter what, she's still our daughter. . . . I, for one, intend to see her through this.

**Wanda:** It's no big deal, Ralph. Lots of people are vegetarians now.

**Ralph:** And a lot of people are Rastafarians and neo-Druids with spiked orange hair. Somehow I thought it was going to pass us by. Maybe I should install a trend alarm that honks wildly whenever a new cult is forming in the neighborhood. I can just hear the neighbors snickering: "There goes poor Ralph; I hear he had to join Lacto-Ovo Parents Anonymous." Why me?

**Ophelia:** You wouldn't get this upset if you cut out the red meat, Dad. You see, your body—

**Ralph:** No dreaded green-bean theology while I'm eating, please, Ophelia. All right. I am braced for a typical parent-child food fight. They come in standard sizes, from pablum-flinging and meat-hating to anorexia. As a matter of fact, a study by Kurt Back, a sociologist at Duke, found that vegetarianism is a favorite form of rebellion among downwardly mobile children of middle-class urban parents. Well, as your father, Ophelia, I am here to say that you can have it all: you can be downwardly mobile AND carnivorous. It's always worked for your mother's side of the family.

**Wanda:** She's not downwardly mobile, Ralph. And she isn't having a food fight. She just doesn't think animals should be tormented, maimed, and killed to keep our stomachs full.

**Ophelia:** Do you like veal, Dad? Calves raised for veal spend all their lives in stalls not much larger than their bodies, without grain to eat or straw to sleep on. Both are sources of iron, and the calves are kept on a painful anemic diet to bring you white and tender veal.

**Ralph:** Stop. I'm having dinner.

**Ophelia:** Or how about eggs? One farmer in New Jersey has eighty thousand laying hens crammed nine each in a cage eighteen inches by twenty-four inches. The hens have no life at all. They never see the outdoors, and the overcrowding creates such stress that the hens have to be debeaked to prevent constant fighting and cannibalism. Or maybe you want to talk about hamburgers? Do you know what the poor cow goes through before dying so you can eat its muscles?

**Ralph:** Not really. Okay. It's safe to stop now. My appetite is now as dead as a former bovine. Ophelia, I grant you that some of the meat and poultry people need to correct a few violations, but does this mean you have to graze through life as a full-time weed-eater? Fad-seeking daughter, you are the splendid genetic result of 10,000 generations of dedicated carnivores. Please do not piddle it away in an orgy of tofu.

**Ophelia:** Omnivores, Dad. Actually, meat only got to be central in our diet fairly recently. Anthropologist Marshall Sahlins says it happened only because of the Indo-European identification of cattle with virility. And Rynn Berry, Jr., in his book *The Vegetarians*, says flesh-eating owes its popularity to the rise of European warrior aristocrats.

**Ralph:** I can see where this is heading: meat-eaters are uppity, bloodthirsty, macho white males—the same folks who brought you Vietnam. Ophelia, as an incipient beansprout guilt-maker, tell me: is the veggie movement actually the sixties recycled, marching for eggplants and chicken lib this time instead of civil rights and peace?

**Ophelia:** It's all very simple, Dad. Meat makes you sick. It can be more lethal than tobacco. It's associated with cancer of the bladder, bowel, skin, lung, stomach, and esophagus. There's also the moral issue of whether we should be raising millions of animals just to impose capital punishment on them all.

**Wanda:** You know, she may have a point, Ralph.

**Ralph:** Wanda, stand by your man! Do not go over to the side of the fashionable carnophobes. Meat-eating is not some murderous trick on the animal world. It's simply our nature, and I refuse to feel guilty about it. Most mammals eat meat. We do not feed our dog lentils.

**Ophelia:** Actually, Dad, you probably could. Many vegetarians feed their dogs a nutritious mix of ground vegetables.

**Ralph:** Talk about animal abuse. Now even our pets have to eat trendy!

**Ophelia:** Among other things, Dad, the meat industry is a very inefficient way of feeding people. First you take grain, which is protein already, put it at great cost into millions of animals, which are then butchered horribly to get the protein back out. Why not eat the grain directly and skip all the waste, pollution, and slaughter?

**Ralph:** Daughter, though smart, you are in the temporary grip of a misty dogma created by sentimental folks who can't see the difference between humans and lower animals. Isaac Bashevis Singer says, "There is only one little step from killing animals to creating gas chambers à la Hitler." Why do I think there may be more of an ethical gap between Adolf and the purchaser of a Roach Motel? Hitler, by the way, was a vegetarian, though he lapsed from the faith when it came to Bavarian sausage. Francis of Assisi, on the other hand, ate meat all the time, slept very well, and never tried to raise dogs on an all-fruit diet. If we ever get a time machine, maybe one of the veggie thought-police should go back and teach him respect for animals.

**Ophelia:** Dad, let me meet you halfway. Yes, this current wave of vegetarianism is vaguely associated with the left, which may drive you to eat nothing but steak from now on. And, yes, there are a few cultish, religious overtones. But you should consider eating less meat, at least. It's better for you, better for the animals. Okay?

**Ralph:** I'll think about it. Now please pass the dismembered cow cadavers.

# Sally Field
# Is Indomitable
# Yet Again

**A**ll of us have seen six or seven indomitable-women movies, but it is not yet fashionable to see them as a genre, like Westerns or kung fu classics. This failure of perception may explain why each new Sally Field movie is given a new title, instead of simply *Norma Rae II, Norma Rae III,* and so forth. Yet the formula is clear enough: an ordinary, domitable woman is pushed by events toward unforeseen strengths and triumph—a distaff version of *Rambo,* minus all the bloody Oriental actors simulating death.

Since men are basically unreliable, and since their presence tends to inhibit indomitability, the heroine to be is fitted out with the basic wimp hubby who cannot come to terms with female success *(Sweet Dreams, Country),* or perhaps with the traditional wife-beater *(Marie, The Color Purple)*. The formula insists that no sane and able-bodied, strong, adult white male (SABSAWM) be found anywhere near the heroine. This is partly because the SABSAWM does not exist, and partly because he would doubtless wreck the plot by flaunting strength and sanity if he did. Since sane sidekicks are important in these movies, the heroine is provided with a stout-hearted lesbian, black, or disabled person to keep her company, admire her rectitude, and stand as a silent rebuke to the morally impoverished (and nonexistent) SABSAWMS.

If the husband has any energy at all in these films, he will devote it to socking his wife or getting shot early on in the action. Otherwise, he just gets to simper, sulk, run away to California, or whine about the latest flood. The real opponents in this genre are Nature and Society. Nature can be counted on to toss a flood, famine, drought, tornado, or tsunami to bring out the steel in the heroine and set the husband blubbering. Society, the repository of all prejudice and meanness, loves to foreclose on family farms and insists that all strong women are sluts. If there are children in the movie, as in all of Sally Field's, she will have to sit them down for a meaningful chat and explain that she is not a slut. There is often a poignant scene which shows the heroine taking her first baby step toward indomitability—perhaps by learning to write a check or pump her own gas.

Despite this, the heroine triumphs most of the time (except when she has to settle for becoming a dead legend by flying into the side of a mountain or getting herself murdered by a major petroleum company). Women prevail; men fail. But to reconcile feminist and family values, the wimp husband is allowed back into the fold as a sheepish junior partner in a new female-headed household.

In case you missed them, here are the rest of the indomitable women films, a much-neglected genre:

*Rosalynn.* The probing tale of a strong-willed Georgia woman married to a diffident peanut farmer who claims he was once president of the United States. Shaken by his wife's success, and depressed by electoral suggestions that he is some sort of wimp, the husband wanders the country aimlessly, and is reported working on a carpentry crew on the Lower East Side. Surviving drought and turbulent peanut prices, the storm-tossed Rosalynn learns that the husband has been calling TV stations at random offering his views on the Middle East. Nevertheless, she takes him back and announces that she will never go hungry again.

*Bonnie and Clyde.* Against a tumultuous backdrop of raging storms and gathering economic forecasts, Clyde develops potency problems related to Bonnie's success in holding up banks. Unfairly attacked as a greedy, thieving slut by narrow-minded bank executives, and frankly bored by Clyde's argument that since guns are phallic symbols men should hold them during stickups, Bonnie voluntarily interrupts her career to soothe the easily threatened male ego. Because of Clyde's instability, so typical of adult white males, Bonnie is forced to adopt a roadside moron as a sidekick. In the climactic scene, societal prejudice against strong women reaches its logical conclusion in a slo-mo machine-gun fusillade—itself a revelation about male violence, as well as a touchingly symbolic echo of Clyde's little problem.

*Mary.* On sheer merit, lovely Mary Cunningham rises in one year from business-school student to the number-two job in a giant corporation. As is always the case with strong women, cruel rumors suggest that Ms. Cunningham is being mentored far into the night by her boss, William Agee. Rightly incensed at charges that she has anything more than a professional relationship with Mr. Agee, the plain-spoken heroine marries him against a backdrop of a raging media shower. Inadvertently swallowed whole during a botched takeover attempt, the bumbling Mr. Agee is nevertheless taken back into the relationship, much like Sam Shepard in *Country.*

*Madonna.* The tale of an energetic New York girl who, despite a singing voice that sounds like Minnie Mouse on helium, becomes a superstar by mistakenly wearing her bra outside her dress. She falls in love with a young actor famous for punching photographers. This requires many court appearances, attracting even more photographers, requiring more punch-outs, and more court appearances, thus, tragically, leaving little time for romance and none for acting. In a scene vaguely reminiscent of the baptism scene in *The Godfather,* Madonna gives birth to a baby as the camera cuts away to her actor-husband, who quickly punches out every photographer in town and retires undefeated.

*Snow White.* Ms. White, dubbed "Snow" for her well-known preference in recreational substances, combats societal prejudice and the ill-founded notion that all women are waiting passively for some kind of prince to come and save them. Able-bodied males are not around, as usual, but with the aid of seven height-disabled yeopersons, Ms. White learns to balance the books on the family diamond mine and refuses poisoned fruit from itinerant bag ladies (themselves victims of societal prejudice). Triumphant, Ms. White ignores the ugly innuendos about her exact relationship with her seven compact roommates. Most touching moment: when Dopey breaks his long silence and asks, "What's a slut, anyway?"

*Fatal Attraction.* This is the end of the indomitable-woman cycle, featuring the crazed but domitable Glenn Close being drowned, stabbed, and shot to death several times as justified punishment for being picked up one weekend by the totally married Michael Douglas. Feminist and family values are both showcased. Feminists get to see men as predatory and unreliable, and family theoreticians get to see the homewrecker-hussy assassinated for fifteen or twenty minutes. And the wife gets to take Michael Douglas back against the background of a very messy bathroom.

# Ralph
# and Wanda
# Fight Fair

**Wanda:** Ralph, my mother is coming to town.

**Ralph:** Where's she staying?

**Wanda:** Right here, insensitive one. Anything wrong with that?

**Ralph:** Nothing at all, my pet, but as it happens, I have to be in Acapulco that week, whenever it is.

**Wanda:** You've always hated my family, Ralph, probably because yours is so lovably flawless—your father who thinks Reagan was a dangerous lefty and your brother the salesman with the spinning bow-tie.

**Ralph:** He spins it once and leaves, Wanda. He doesn't stay here ten or twelve days pointing out child-rearing deficiencies, hairline cracks in the ceiling, and herbal flaws in the soup.

**Wanda:** That's my mother you're attacking, Ralph. You're never nice to her or any of my friends.

**Ralph:** Don't say never, Wanda, I've warned you a million times about hyperbole. And don't raise your voice while I am lecturing you.

**Wanda:** Subside, Ralph. Mother isn't coming. I staged this argument to make a point.

**Ralph:** I have the feeling, my dearest, that I'm about to hear of still another breakthrough in the annals of self-help techniques.

**Wanda:** Correct, Ralph. It's called fair-fighting theory, and counselors and therapists use it all the time. Remember how I escalated our argument from my mother to your family and my friends? That's called "gunnysacking," saving up resentments and spewing them out to cloud the debate.

**Ralph:** I assume we must stick logically to the point, as the male mind inclines your average husband to do.

**Wanda:** We must also avoid stereotypes, Ralph, though I realize this will be a hardship for you. You can't say "You women . . . ," "Typical female," or use cosmic phrases such as "I know you, Wanda," or "You don't listen to me." These are illegal punches.

**Ralph:** Does that include "You don't love me anymore" and "If you loved me you'd know what's bothering me"?

**Wanda:** Absolutely, contentious one. Fair fighters don't expect their partners to divine their problems through mystic revelation. They tell them. Psychologizing—tossing out cocktail-party Freudian insights—is not allowed either. The point is that every marriage is a complaint factory, and sensible couples learn to thrash things out in a nonpoisonous way. It might help if we considered having some arguments in front of trusted friends.

**Ralph:** You've got some experience there, dearest. Remember the time you waited until Walter and Cathy were just about to leave our car, then delivered your ghastly diatribe about my death-defying driving? I was all stoked up for a peachy rebuttal, but they couldn't hang around to hear it.

**Wanda:** That's called delving into the psychiatric museum, Ralph: dredging up a long-treasured injustice. It's okay to argue reasonably in front of your friends, but I was wrong to badger you in front of them. Your correct response would have been "Ouch."

**Ralph:** "Ouch?"

**Wanda:** That signals an illegal punch. It alerts the offending partner to get back on track without escalating things. A stronger signal is "Foul" for a below-the-belt punch, one aimed at some known vulnerability, like your wig.

**Ralph:** Ouch and foul. It's a hairpiece. Howard Cosell has a wig. I—

**Wanda:** Never mind that, Ralph. There's an emergency signal, too, when one partner feels threatened. It can be "Stop," "You win," or any code word at all. It's like the baring of the throat that stops a wolf fight. Also you can negotiate pauses or ends of rounds in any fight. I might say, "Do you have everything off your chest now?" That means, if we have both had our say and reached no agreement, let's stop awhile and pick it up later. Now, if you really want to have a fair fight, the standard opening is "I've got a bone to pick with you."

**Ralph:** Okay. I've got a bone to pick with you.

**Wanda:** Good so far, Ralph. Pick away.

**Ralph:** My bone is this: Why is it that we have to incorporate into our marriage every idea that slithers out of Southern California?

**Wanda:** Oh, Ralph, not again. Why do you always resist new ideas so stubbornly? They're not germs, you know.

**Ralph:** Cosmic statement, Wanda. Out of bounds. You never really listen.

**Wanda:** Illegal comment. Are you so threatened by the idea of fair fights because you might have to give up your Vesuvian monologues?

**Ralph:** Gunnysacking and psychologizing. Wanda, have I ever pointed out that you argue like your mother?

**Wanda:** Ouch. Foul. Ralph, if this argument goes one second further, I'm going to scream.

**Ralph:** Stop. You win, Wanda. Nice fight, wasn't it?

**Wanda:** It really cleared the air. Let's eat.

# SEX
# IN THE
# EIGHTIES:
# A SHORT
# HISTORY

# The
# Babe Ruth
# of Sex

**Wanda:** It's ten o'clock, Ralph. Do you want the news or the Ruth Westheimer show?

**Ralph:** One vote here for prurience, my sweet. Who wants to watch withering drought and death-dealing heat waves when you can switch to radio and hear Debbie from Saskatoon describing her woefully low genital sensitivity? How can conflict in the Persian Gulf compare with Rosalie of Omaha asking Dr. Ruth which porno films to flash on the ceiling while locked in the clumsy embrace of husband Bob, the rapid-fire mortician?

**Wanda:** No need to be so sarcastic, Ralph. Ruth is good at what she does. I take it you don't like her.

**Ralph:** Far from it, light of my life. She's my favorite sex munchkin, the correct answer to the riddle "What's fifty-five inches long and sexually useful?" Who else would tackle the tough question of whether a devout Catholic like Bruce from Dubuque shows disrespect for his church by doing it dressed as a nun? These are the very issues they duck all the time on *Face the Nation* and *Meet the Press.*

**Wanda:** Try to subside, dearest. Dr. Ruth must be doing something right. *Sexually Speaking,* her radio call-in show, has been on the air for more than ten years. She has a syndicated late-night TV show, her cable show, a syndicated newspaper column, videocassettes, Dr. Ruth games, and all the rest. She's everywhere.

**Ralph:** And no wonder, my pet. Chicken soup and voyeurism are a dynamic combination. You could spend a decade peering into the neighbors' bedroom windows and not get half the kick of a Westheimer show. You sit mesmerized as Ruth soothingly points out, "Normalcy is hard to define," and "There is no one right size for the penis." You get to look down on all the bumpkins who call in wondering whether Ben-Gay makes them sterile. In fact, everything's such a mess out there, it makes your own sex life seem pretty good. I hasten to add that ours is superb, by the way. Best of all, my beloved one, when you listen to Dr. Ruth, you feel a surge of therapeutic uplift that many of us find to be missing from your average porno film. So you don't have to feel slimy at all when you hear what Yvonne of Tucson does with the Cool Whip. What more can you ask from a talk show?

**Wanda:** I'm surprised you don't have a bit more sympathy for her, Ralph. Actually, she's rather conservative. She doesn't think married people should fool around. She says people should keep the rules of their religion and should feel guilty when they do rotten things. That's enough to set her apart from a good many people in the sex-advice business. She doesn't even think people should have sex on the first date.

**Ralph:** A sexual conservative who dispenses soft-core porn will never go broke in America, dearest.

**Wanda:** Give her a little credit, Ralph. She's funny, and she has a knack for relaxing all those troubled people out there. She told one couple to go to a motel to refresh their sex life. The woman called back later to report that nothing had happened, and Ruth said, "Well, at least you had a good night's sleep." Her advice is sensible. She tells people to be romantic and realistic too—sexual appetite waxes and wanes even in the best relationships. Believe it or not, she also advises people to be careful about sharing details of their sex lives. She talks about one man who admitted to an encounter group that he was turned on whenever he saw a cow. The group was bound by secrecy, but when the poor fellow got to his office, his secretary and everyone else began calling out "Moo! Moo!"

**Ralph:** If everybody were as reticent as she seems to advise, she would have no show, dearest. Thanks to the good Dr. Ruth, thousands of otherwise normal people are happy to go on the air to discuss the configuration of their spouses' private parts. Next thing you know, we will all be using one another's toothbrushes, Wanda.

**Wanda:** We live in a sexually frank age, Ralph. She's using that frankness to help people.

**Ralph:** A cynic might say she is using a marketable schtick, Wanda. Your dowager aunt can be counted on to ask about the children, but Ruth—looking so tiny, wholesome, and middle-aged—leans forward sweetly and asks you what setting you use on your five-speed vibrator. It's a brilliant effect, a variation of about forty familiar dirty jokes. It wouldn't work at all if she were a normal size, or if she looked and sounded sexy. Apart from two or three of those sharp comments per show, she has the wit to play the straight man. She knows people tune in for the lurid tales from the provinces and not just to hear her say, "Have you tried masturbation?" or "Why don't you do it in the kitchen?"

**Wanda:** Somehow, Ralph, I get the impression that no program on sex could ever meet your standards.

**Ralph:** I've got it, Wanda! Why don't I just take over the Westheimer show and give it some class? I'll call it *Ask Dr. Ralph* or *Orgasmically Speaking,* something upscale and tony like that. Horny housewives and bored cabbies can tune in as I deftly field anguished queries from Marvin of Hackensack, whose penis apparently swivels too much to the left, and Elsie of Batavia, who cannot achieve the Big O unless there's a trained chimp in the room. Naturally, I would take the high ground, quelling all this genital turmoil by declaring everyone normal, including the chimp, and instructing all listeners to "Go for it!" —with safe-sex contraceptives, of course. I would then startle my rapt audience by revealing that sex is nothing to be ashamed of, that in fact it may even be a natural part of life. Then as a finale, I would beam at my audience, looking sweet while talking dirty. What do you think, my partner in love as well as life?

**Wanda:** I think it's time to go to bed, Ralph.

**Ralph:** Right, dearest. You start. Dr. Ruth will get us through this in a jiffy.

# The Return of the Sexual Squares

**Wanda:** Ralph, do you remember Stanley, who ran off with the meter maid and joined the love commune in Altoona? Well, it seems he's back with his wife again.

**Ralph:** What happened, dearest? Fear of AIDS? Or did she come into some money?

**Wanda:** Try not to be cynical so early in a conversation, Ralph. Stanley just wanted to explore his sensuality. Once he did, he came to see that an in-depth relationship with one person is more challenging and erotic than casual sex with many.

**Ralph:** Poor Stanley. He'll have to do some remedial reading of the revolutionary texts. Didn't Alex Comfort tell us in *More*

*Joy of Sex* that "hot sex" with its "tragic intensities" was far inferior to cool, unemotional sex?

**Wanda:** That was in the seventies, Ralph. We are way beyond that now. Many people tried to detach sex from love back then, but that was because society told them they couldn't have one without the other. Now that society has relaxed a bit—

**Ralph:** Wanda, you're trying to bring me a bulletin from the sexual frontier. Out with it.

**Wanda:** Commitment is in, Ralph.

**Ralph:** You mean sex is not just a user-friendly technology? Tell me more.

**Wanda:** Nowadays we speak of intimacy, pair bonding, working at relationships. In sexuality, quality is more important than quantity. There's a big reaction against the trivialization of sex. George Leonard, who used to be a guru at Esalen, has written a new book called *The End of Sex,* and it talks about the ideal of "high monogamy." Anything wrong with that, curmudgeon of mine?

**Ralph:** Nothing at all, my pet. Fresh cant is an important component in America's never-ending quest for novelty. What is high monogamy, by the way? I assume I have been a notably low monogamist all these years.

**Wanda:** One of the lowest, my stodgy one. High monogamy is people staying together, not because they have to but because they know who they are and because they want what Leonard calls "challenge and an adventure." He talks about "two vibrant entities merging to become a new vibrancy."

**Ralph:** Sounds awfully shaky to me, dearest. Two vibrating people in one small apartment might be enough to drive Stanley back to Altoona. What other news from the front?

**Wanda:** Living together is not seen as a rejection of marriage anymore. It's more of a way station, almost part of the courtship ritual. And divorce ends in remarriage so routinely that you could call it a backhanded compliment to marriage and its claims.

**Ralph:** This is certainly bracing news for us lovemongers, Wanda. If stability and commitment are the watchwords, then I take it that the sexual revolution is over?

**Wanda:** Yes, it's over, Ralph, because it has been won. There are just a few counterrevolutionary guerrillas like you and Jerry Falwell left up there in the hills.

**Ralph:** Harsh words, Wanda. Have I ever uttered a single word against the sainted cause of the revolution?

**Wanda:** No, but I have a feeling you will.

**Ralph:** Far from it, beloved helpmate. In fact, I grow nostalgic for the cause. Who will ever forget the jolly sex communes, the fantasy workshops and masturbation classes, the reading thrill of each new episode of *Playboy* philosophy, and the dedicated search for new female sex organs? Remember the wellspring of sympathy for "erotic minorities" (aka perverts), and the invention of "creative divorce," leading to "quality time" of forty-five minutes a week spent with the kids during that important self-actualizing period after a creative divorce? Then there's your cousin Bruce down in Greenwich Village. He stayed an extra five years with his wife waiting for the inevitable fulfillment of Alex Comfort's prediction that bisexuality would be "standard middle-class morality" by 1984. I think he knew your friend Marvin who nearly got himself gelded in a sex-change operation because he considered himself a woman trapped in a man's body, when actually, he later concluded, he was merely a dentist trapped in Chicago. I believe he is now into yoga, a pursuit which luckily requires no genital mutilation at all. Ah, Wanda! Those were the days!

**Wanda:** You argue quite fluently for a deranged person, Ralph. I suppose we were all better off back in your favorite decade, the fifties, the golden age of shotgun weddings, coat-hanger abortions, and wall-to-wall guilt. Everybody but you and Cotton Mather knows that there is more frankness, spontaneity, and joy in sex because of the changes. Even a Cro-Magnon philosopher like yourself should have no trouble opposing that. Why do you judge the sexual revolution by its most frivolous people, as if the whole idea were to set up a nationwide game of chase-the-meter-maid or jump-the-stewardess?

**Ralph:** I believe you meant to say "flight attendant," dearest. Actually I am thrilled to see marriage and commitment making a comeback among the self-realizers, Californicators, and middle-aged kids left over from the sixties. There is nothing so touching as watching someone reinvent the wheel.

**Wanda:** None of your diatribes would be complete without a shot at the sixties. Can I assume you are winding down?

**Ralph:** Absolutely, and if I may sum up, there is much to be said on both sides, including a bit of yours. But since we spent the revolutionary period together, Wanda, I have a question. . . .

**Wanda:** Yes, recalcitrant one?

**Ralph:** Was it good for you too?

**Wanda:** See me later, Ralph. Right now, I'm working on a headache.

# Searching High and Low for the Big O

**Ralph:** Quiz time, dearest. What moves around more often than Elizabeth Taylor, the *QE2,* and the wandering albatross?

**Wanda:** I give up, Ralph. What?

**Ralph:** The female orgasm. In the old days, it used to be in the vagina. Then they shipped it to the clitoris, where it remained stationary for a decade. Now it seems to be on the move again. Just restless, I guess.

**Wanda:** Ralph, what on earth are you talking about?

**Ralph:** The Great Traveling Orgasm, my pet. Under the majestic scepter of science, not to mention the cattle prod of sexual politics, the Big O is thrashing about once again. It's gone from vagina to clitoris and now seems headed for the brain and back to the vagina. Before you know it, it will come to rest on the elbow or the pancreas. *Ralph's Guide to Sex,* as yet unpublished, will advise all ardent males to rub everything once. One never knows where tomorrow's sexual climaxes will be located.

**Wanda:** I am about to have an out-of-body experience, Ralph. But I suppose I could remain here with you and your monologue if a fact or two happens to intrude.

**Ralph:** Facts are the backbone of good argument, my beloved. I hold here in my hand the current winter issue of the *Journal of Sex and Marital Therapy.* And I quote, "From recent empirical studies it can be concluded that most (and probably all) women possess vaginal zones whose tactile stimulation can lead to orgasm." Apparently the long tyranny of the clitoris is coming to an end, dearest. At least until the next dramatic breakthrough of sexual science or the next long-awaited wave of fearlessly ferocious feminism.

**Wanda:** You argue like a rogue elephant running downhill, Ralph. Look, Masters and Johnson showed that the clitoral-vaginal debate was irrelevant. There is only one kind of orgasm, and it almost always involved stimulation of the clitoris. It's just that orgasms without that stimulation are rarer and milder than those with it.

**Ralph:** Bravely argued, my pet. But let us cast a practiced eye at the politics of orgasm. Freud thought that truly mature women always shift their focus from the clitoris to the vagina, so women who needed clitoral stimulation were made to feel like retards or perverts. The feminists just reversed that. It was a much-loved way of downgrading penis-vagina sex and upgrading masturbation, which, after all, doesn't require the presence of an actual male. Soon pro-vagina women had to take to the hills like guerrillas. Clitoral enforcers like Shere Hite were sent out to mop up any remaining opposition: the poor deluded women who said they had vaginal orgasms and thought they were enjoying them. Hite called this "emotional" orgasm, as opposed to "real orgasm." The clitoro-feminists also managed to clear out the compromisers, who believed in "blended" vaginal-clitoral orgasms. What the heck. It worked for Scotch, why not for climaxes? But no, the clitoral-pride movement took over. For all we know, women who used to fake vaginal orgasms for their hubbies began to fake clitoral ones for the women's movement. I guess you could call this progress of a sort. But do women really have to limit themselves to politically correct orgasms? Wanda, I stand before you as that rarest of males, a true feminist, calling for relief from the dogmas of Freudians and clitorists alike!

**Wanda:** I liked you better as a chauvinist pig, benighted husband of mine. Your argument has only one minor flaw, Ralph: it's totally wrong. There is no clitoral party line, though easily threatened males may think so. The clitoris is the normal center of women's sexuality, and it is not our fault that it happens to be located in a spot that men find inconvenient. I bet that the article in the *Journal of Sex and Marital Therapy* is just more wool-gathering about the G-spot.

**Ralph:** Wrong, beloved helpmate. In fact, the author of the journal's piece, a sexologist named Heli Alzate, says that his own studies show no evidence of any such sexually sensitive tissue in the vaginal wall where the G-spot is alleged to be. These are dark days for G-spotologists, my dear. Ernst Gräfenberg discovered his spot in the late forties. But after many exhausting years in the lab stimulating all those hired prostitutes and cutting up all those cadavers, there's still no convincing evidence. But then, sexology is not an exact science. Who says they should be able to locate a major sexual organ after only forty years of searching? Anyway the G-spot people say the sensitive spot is usually found between eleven o'clock and one o'clock on the vaginal barrel. Alzate thinks there may be two other hot spots, at four o'clock and eight o'clock.

**Wanda:** Why do I find all this so tacky? All these white-coated males poking around the female body, checking the wiring and looking for new buttons to push. Why are you all so obsessed with the technology of women's bodies?

**Ralph:** Easy there, Wanda. It's just that males found out where their orgasms were located a million years ago, and women are still working on it. No problem. They'll probably figure it out any day now.

**Wanda:** Let me tell you a little secret, Ralph. I married a lout. Who cares about the technology of orgasm? Sex is supposed to be part of a relationship, not a high-school biology course. Some women have orgasms without contractions, and the white coats smile down and say, "Sorry, we can't count those because we can't measure them." Same old stuff of males using science to define and control women.

**Ralph:** Mellow out, dearest. Surely an acknowledged feminist such as myself is not the enemy. . . .

**Wanda:** I'm developing a blinding headache in my R spot. That's the dwindling section of my brain that thinks you're rational, Ralph. This headache is fully located between nine P.M. and six A.M. on both my clock and my cranial barrel. For further information on the status of this headache, phone me in a week. Thank you and good night.

# No
# F-Words,
# Please

**Dear Ms. Morals:** While watching the World Series, I noticed that Dodger manager Tommy Lasorda uses the F-word an awful lot. Is this a good thing?

**Dear Concerned:** You are a very observant fan. Yes, Tommy is fond of this word. There's a tape of him using it twenty-eight times while removing pitcher Bob Welch during the 1981 World Series. At that rate, with two pitching changes per game, Lasorda would emit about ten thousand F-words per season just while standing on the mound. You can imagine what life in the dugout is like. Close friends tell us that Tommy knows many other words. It's just that he can't seem to think of any of them while he is speaking. But what a season he had! And remem-

SEX IN THE EIGHTIES: A SHORT HISTORY

ber, the F-word is an accepted part of baseball. Author Lenny Dykstra of the Mets uses it a hundred sixty times in his book *Nails,* and as you know, he is a fine center fielder, though the Mets lost to Lasorda in the play-offs.

**Dear Ms. Morals:** Thanks for straightening me out about baseball, but now I am concerned about rock music. Do we have to have so many songs with the F-word in the title and lyrics, or is this necessary to get across the singers' authentic feelings about rape and torture? Am I being old-fashioned about this?

**Dear Tipper:** I am afraid so. Let's face facts. Rock singers may not be rocket scientists, but you probably go too far calling them mutants and foul little snots. As you know, these artists are under constant pressure to irritate parents like you. This is what rock musicians are for. Remember, the F-word is an accepted part of their culture, just as politeness is part of yours. The same person who sent us the Lasorda tape sent us one of the Troggs rehearsing. In five minutes there were seventy F-words and several bars of music. Take away the F-word and there would have been silence. Is that what you want from rock?

**Dear Ms. Morals:** You have me there. I can see now that I am far too judgmental. But what about movies, or perhaps I should say cinema. Movies like *Midnight Run* and *Scarface* numb you with F-assaults. I enjoy going to the movies and frankly I am tired of seeing *Bambi* all the time. I took my kids to see *Adventures in Babysitting.* Since it's basically a lollipop movie for the preteen set, I thought it would be safe, but, no, it's loaded with the F-word. What's a parent to do?

**Dear Concerned:** Try to lighten up. Hollywood is just going through an F-word phase, and you should think of it as one big troubled adolescent. F-word experts like Oliver Stone and Marty Scorcese are trying to reinvigorate the industry with lots of manly invective. The little joke in Hollywood is that Oliver Stone gets ten thousand dollars per F-word, the word he knows how to type best. As you can see, this is far more than Lasorda would make at the same rate, and quite near Eddie Murphy's pay, which is higher because he wisely specializes in compound participles. As for *Adventures in Babysitting,* perhaps you should be asking yourself, Is a movie theater the right place for my child?

**Dear Ms. Morals:** Good point. Okay. I am willing to write off baseball, movies, guitar-bangers, stand-up comedy, army sergeants, David Mamet, and tapes of Richard Nixon in the White House. But now an article in *Spy* Magazine by Mark Lasswell tells me that a whole bunch of magazines are throwing the F-word around, including *The New Yorker.* Is this the end or something? I thought *The New Yorker* used to stand for decorum and taste. Should Eustace Tilly be going BLEEP all over the place?

**Dear Concerned:** Standards are nice, but you must get with it and accept your culture. Embrace it whole. Take Robert Stone. He holds the current F-word record at *The New Yorker* with one *f,* two *f——ers,* four *f——in's,* and three *f——ings,* all in one short story. Do you want his high-testosterone heroes to grow purple with rage and then shout, "Heck!"? Of course not. If Shakespeare and Hemingway were alive today, they would doubtless be f——ing it in *The New Yorker* along with Veronica Geng and all the other macho types. Arthur Gelb of *The New*

*York Times* says Harold Ross, the founding editor of *The New Yorker,* is very likely spinning in his grave. In fairness, there is no real way to tell what, if anything, Harold Ross is doing just now. And you must remember that Gelb is speaking as a *Times* man and the *Times* is still stuck in its pre-F-word stage. I can tell you this. William Shawn introduced the word, but the new editor, Robert Gottlieb, is presiding over the golden age of F. "I find————a much more disturbing word than *f————ing,*" is the way he puts it. He has no policy on the F-word, just the opinion that "It's a shame that such a happy sexual word should have become so aggressive."

**Dear Ms. Morals:** I am beginning to lose the thread of this and I am running out of stamps. A Perry Ellis ad last year contained the phrase *f————k you,* and T-shirts with the entire F-word are being worn to school by many teenagers who have been told by the ACLU that this is what the Founding Fathers had in mind. I know you are going to tell me that the F-word is an accepted part of advertising and T-shirt manufacture, but my question is this: Is it still safe to turn on my television set?

**Dear Concerned:** Now that the networks have eliminated their standards-and-practices offices, no one can say for sure. But remember, ours is a vital, rapidly changing, and infinitely adaptable culture, constantly shedding the dead skin of the past, including people like you, you f—ing prude.We hope this is of some help. Please write us anytime and have a nice day.

# BASEBALL, BIRDING, AND BLOWHARDS

# How the Russians Invented Baseball

Sergei Shachin, citing cultural historians, insists that baseball descended from an ancient Russian game of bats and balls called lapta, brought by Russian émigrés to what is now California some two centuries before the arrival of the Dodgers and Giants.

Lapta is a folk game in which the batter swats a ball tossed gently in front of him by a teammate. Then he tries to run across a field before an opponent can fetch the ball and hit the runner with it.

"Baseball is the younger brother of lapta," Mr. Shachin explained to the eight million readers of Izvestia. ". . . It's just a shame that we allowed lapta to be undeservedly forgotten, while baseball fans were aggressively promoting it."

—THE NEW YORK TIMES, JULY 20, 1987

Although some Americans seem a bit skeptical about the recent news that Russians invented baseball, or lapta, as it has been known for the last sixty or seventy Soviet pennant races, the matter is old hat to knowledgeable sports fans. As *Izvestia* recently explained to its readers, Russian émigrés brought the game to what is now California two hundred years ago, with batters striking at a ball with a stick, and fielders throwing the ball (a rock) at opposition players to register outs.

The Russian origin of American baseball is a simple fact and a closed issue, but Soviet Leader Mikhail Gorbachev, jocularly dubbed "Goose Glasnost" by the Professional Lapta Writers Association, has graciously allowed speculation on how the game actually got to America. *Pravda* believes it was stolen by a Marine guard at the U.S. embassy in Moscow who scurrilously wheedled crucial lapta information out of an unwary Russian cook during an evening of illicit and probably drug-induced lovemaking sometime in the eighteen forties.

Another school of thought holds that the game arose in the tenth century, and was brought to America by one of the earliest people's explorers, Eric the Red, who is said to have founded a team named for himself in what is now Cincinnati. Other equally respected laptologists maintain that the spirited game evolved from the famous sporting rides of the cossacks. In this view, games occurred spontaneously on the Russian steppes, with peasants hurling stones up at the fabled horsemen in attempts to achieve outs, while the free-swinging cossacks, many of them boasting nine- or ten-village hitting streaks, were responsible for most of the offense. The amazing success of the cossacks, who often went undefeated for decades at a time, is sometimes cited by *Izvestia* as proof that polo as well as baseball originated in sports-minded Russia. It also helps explain why so many modern Russians show up for work every Monday morning proudly displaying full-body lapta bruises.

This pro-Cossack school generally aligns itself with the West Coast theory of American baseball. In this opinion, the first American team was not the Cincinnati Reds, but the Los Angeles Engels, named for the wealthy crony who liked to toss the lapta around with Karl Marx, the game's greatest theoretician and the main reason why so many modern lapta stars have been nicknamed "Lefty." Marx and Engels introduced the dialectical theory of lapta: the pitchers are always ahead of the hitters, and vice versa. Marx's classic one-liner about lapta, "Nice right-wing deviationists finish last," ranks with Lenin's famous admonition about the Russian psyche: "Anyone who wishes to understand the Russian soul had better learn lapta."

It was Lenin, in fact, who called for expansion of the Russian national pastime from a stagnant game merely played east of the Urals to one that offered its excitement to a waiting world. The historic postwar expansion brought coveted major-league franchises to such cities as Warsaw, Prague, and Budapest, where local sportsmen, eager to learn the new game, playfully threw a great many welcoming laptas at the arriving Russian players. The game even reached Kabul, where enthusiastic Afghan players dramatically altered traditional notions of defense by using the first heat-seeking laptas during regular season play. Much like the introduction of the corked bat and the designated hitter in the U.S., the Afghan innovation clearly irritated a few hidebound older fans back in Moscow, who talked constantly of "lowering the mound" in mountainous Afghanistan to bring offense and defense back into classic balance.

Over the centuries, lapta has developed many colorful customs and expressions. For instance, the peasant who had only one lapta in hand, but two cossacks bearing down on him, was said to be confronting a "fielder's choice." Third base has been known as "the hot corner" since the Minsk-Pinsk World Series of 1937, when a Pinsk third-base coach, who happened to double as a political-education instructor, repeatedly harassed the Minsk third baseman with probing theoretical questions. Tragically, this led to the only fatality in big-league lapta. During the seventh game of the Series, after uttering the ill-advised suggestion "Stick it in your ear, comrade coach," the luckless Minsk third baseman was dragged from the Cosmodome by large men in bulky suits, executed, and later brought to trial.

Unlike capitalist versions of the game, lapta does not permit base-stealing, since the bases belong to all the people and cannot be appropriated for individual use. Sacrifices, on the other hand, are encouraged, and often occur even with no runners on base. Instead of a left, center, and right fielder, the typical lapta outfield will feature two left fielders followed around by a fleet fellow traveler, or perhaps yet another British free agent eager to play ball with the Russians.

Diehard lapta fans bitterly resented President Reagan's recent remark about the Soviets' "evil umpires." In truth, umpires are so revered in the Soviet Union that players often call out, "Honor to the umpires!" and managers run out of the dugouts to congratulate the men in blue on successfully making difficult calls. This is because the umpires are scrupulously fair and usually have close relatives on the party's Central Committee.

They are also famous for appreciating a good joke. One was told by the illustrious star Lefty Jabov, who once hit eighty-nine homers in a single year, more than Babe Ruth, Roger Maris, or other inferior Americans weakened by decades of debilitating capitalist exploitation of the toiling masses. After a called third strike, the fun-loving slugger turned to the beloved umpire and quipped, "But, comrade, Marx said that when workers controlled the means of production, there would be no more strikes!" The joke was considered so funny that Jabov was not jailed at all, merely sent down to the Siberian League for a brief attitudinal readjustment.

As it happens, the slugger's seven-foot-tall younger brother, Kareem Jabov, is a famous Soviet sports figure in his own right. Shortly after the Russian invention of soccer, the gangly Kareem picked up a soccer ball and playfully thrust it back over his head into a potato basket hanging from the rafter of a people's barn, thus simultaneously inventing both the in-your-face reverse slam dunk and the entire game of basketball. But that is another story. Watch for it soon in the pages of *Izvestia*.

# Keep
# Irish Meusel
# Out Of
# Cooperstown

**A**rguments about mediocre ballplayers in the Hall of Fame come up all the time. When they do, I always think of the term Tom Hoving dreamed up while delicately selling off some minor paintings at the Metropolitan Museum. Instead of announcing that he was cleaning some junk out of the attic, Hoving told the press he was merely "deaccessioning" a few works the museum no longer needed.

What a great word! Every baseball fan knows that the Hall of Fame desperately needs a touch of Hoving's genius for removing unwanted museum pieces with minimum fuss. Who wouldn't like to deaccession players like Sunny Jim Bottomley, Zack Wheat, Jesse Haines, Chick Hafey, or George Kell, who was mistakenly accessioned a few years ago by the perennially woeful veterans committee?

Who would shed a single tear if Tom "The Deaccessor" Hoving became commissioner and quietly cleared out a few cartloads of other embarrassing acquisitions such as Enos Slaughter, Earl Averill, Stanley Coveleski, Eppa Rixey, Rick Ferrell, and Lloyd (but not Paul) Waner?

Rabbit Maranville was a decent shortstop, but he is in the Hall only because he happened to play for the 1914 Miracle Braves. Toss him out. Ray Schalk is a baseball immortal mostly because he was not in on the plot by his Black Sox teammates to throw the 1919 World Series. But then lots of players never threw a World Series. Out. Roger Bresnahan was a perfectly adequate though occasionally self-destructive catcher. He is really in the Hall because he introduced two useful gadgets, the catcher's mask and the shin guard. Does this mean we have to vote Steve Yeager in for inventing the little mask-flap that protects the catcher's Adam's apple? What about the guy who bought the first resin bag or corked the first bat? Out. Out. Out.

Most of the folly, maybe ninety percent of the truly demented selections, comes from the committee on veterans. Each year when the committee votes, informed fans can usually be found under their beds, awaiting another dread announcement that somebody like Tookie Gilbert or Marv Throneberry has just been declared a baseball immortal.

The committee is now busy inducting all the remaining midlevel players of the twenties, thirties, and forties. They stuffed Kiki Cuyler and Hack Wilson into the Hall, and now there's a boom for the last member of that Cub outfield, Riggs Stephenson, who doesn't belong in there either.

If whole outfields, why not whole teams? The following members of the 1925–1926 New York Giants are now in the Hall: first base—Bill Terry and George Kelly; second base—Frankie Frisch and Rogers Hornsby; shortstop—Travis Jackson; third base—Freddie Lindstrom; outfield—Mel Ott, Hack Wilson, and Ross Youngs.

You would think that with all those amazing titans around, the Giants would never have lost a game. But somehow, perhaps unaware of their total group greatness, they won no pennants at all for eight years.

Since the Giants of that period practically have their own wing at Cooperstown, here's a trivia question: Name the only man who played more than 162 games for the '25–'26 Giants and is NOT in the Hall of Fame. Answer: Irish Meusel. But stay tuned. One more wave of sentiment and log-rolling on the veterans committee and Irish will sweep right in, with Riggs Stephenson right on his heels.

The committee was set up in the late thirties because officials thought that the regular voters, the baseball writers, were too young to remember turn-of-the-century stars. Logically, then, the committee should have disbanded after five or ten years, since the turn of the century isn't getting any closer. Now all it does is second-guess the real voters and recycle rejects. Worst of all, nothing is ever settled. Presumably we will have twenty more years of the fuss over Rizzuto. Unless the committee relents so it won't have to listen to sixty more of those between-the-innings television chats that begin: "Say, Scooter, how come you're not in the Hall of Fame?"

The real reason to put the committee to sleep, however, is not that it is doing a wretched job, but that there is no job left to do. The Macmillan *Baseball Encyclopedia* has been out for more than eighteen years with a complete statistical record. We know how to weigh and adjust those stats for the era and the ballparks that everyone played in. Researchers have interviewed the old stars, pored over old newspaper reports, and analyzed MVP voting, All-Star selections, and trade data. This process has been so exhaustive that it can now be said flatly: there are no great old-time ballplayers left for the Veterans Committee to enshrine. Say good-night, committee members.

The baseball writers have their own Hall of Fame concerns. Let's call it the Drysdale problem. Don Drysdale was an outstanding pitcher for a long time, clearly better than ten or twelve pitchers already in the hall, but he was not a pitcher of the first rank like Marichal and Koufax. It was not a disgrace to put him in, as the writers did in 1984, but now they face the usual downward spiral. If Drysdale is in, why not Lew Burdette, Jim Bunning, Mickey Lolich, and other pitchers with similar stats? If that group goes in, you will hear the drums beat for Luis Tiant, Hal Newhouser, Billy Pierce, and Paul Derringer. Do we want every good pitcher in the hall, or just the great ones?

As Bill James, author of the *Baseball Abstract,* points out, the spiral never works the other way. Nobody ever says, "If Rizzuto isn't in, let's take Reese out" or "We can't put Bobby Doerr in because Tony Lazzeri and Joe Gordon aren't there." Or how about the down spiral based on Koufax's short career: if six great years put him in the hall, in a career cut short by injuries, what about the five great years of Denny McLain, whose career was cut short by felonies?

One more point to harangue the baseball writers about.

Please try to overcome the fascination with 500 (as in home runs) and 300 (as in wins). Dave Kingman is a truly terrible ballplayer. His typical year is 25 homers, 50 singles, 175 strikeouts, one season-long sullen and lethargic attitude, and 15 or 20 bonehead plays. If one year like that is awful, why would 20 of them strung together (adding up to 500 home runs) make him a Hall of Famer?

Like the $100,000 house, the 300-win total is not what it used to be, but the voting is unlikely to take account of the inflation brought about by longer careers. Don Sutton, for example, is going into the hall for winning 300 games. Yes, he is a good pitcher—a solid but unspectacular ERA compiled in pitcher-friendly parks; he led the league in ERA once and won 20 once. Nothing special there. He spent almost all of his career as his team's number-three or number-two starter, almost never as the ace of his own staff. This is a Hall of Famer? No one thought so during his prime. No one would think so now except for the obsession with the number 300.

Rule Number One for Hall of Fame voting in the nineties: Hanging around a long time does not produce greatness, only large numbers. Even the sabremetricians, the numbers-crunchers of baseball who have done so much of the important research, seem much too smitten by the mileage a team gets out of a player. Okay. Sutton gave good mileage. He is a solid Chevy that surprised its many owners by lasting 125,000 miles. But the hall is for Mercedes and Rolls-Royces. This means Gibson, Seaver, Carlton, Koufax, and Marichal. Not Niekro, Kaat, Sutton, and Bunning, and certainly not Nolan Ryan, unless you want to open a new side gallery for exciting .500

pitchers and stash him there with Bobo Newsom and Wilbur Wood.

Finally, in the spirit of the great Tom Hoving, baseball must gather its wits and decide to have regular recall elections to remove the mistakes from the hall. One suggestion is that it require eighty-five percent of the vote by the writers, balloting only on deceased members of the hall. Don't be shocked. It will have to come someday. Remember, people once thought that any painting bought by the Met would be there forever too. And it isn't just deaccessioning either. Every once in a while, some expert comes along and decides that some ten-million-dollar Rembrandt is really a fake, and out it goes. Can we do less with Eppa Rixey?

# Spanky
# Predicts a
# Pennant Race

**A**s all true baseball fans know, the news from spring training these days is heavily financial and pharmaceutical. Yet another losing pitcher has signed for millions. Free agents are still being locked out. One more slugger will make a wobbly attempt to face the world without the help of controlled substances. But beneath all those grim reports of labor wrangling, detoxed relief pitchers, and random urine tests, the sharp-eyed fan can usually turn up an item or two that pertains to the actual game of baseball itself. One of the most cherished is the traditional interview with the big-league manager on the probable fortunes of his team. As the warm Florida (or Arizona) suns beats down, the exchange customarily goes like this:

**Baseball reporter:** "How's the squad gonna do this year, Spanky?"

**Manager:** "This is a scrappy, hustling team, Vinnie. (Expectorates.) If we can get off to a good start and everybody stays healthy, anything can happen. (Renewed expectoration.) I can tell you one thing"—shifts tobacco to other cheek—"we'll be heard from before this thing is over."

Spanky has just given a world-class prediction. It is emphatic, hedged in a manly, determined way; and yet, to satisfy demanding reporters, it remains almost totally content-free. The key to success is to keep things heartily vague. Second-division managers like to go around saying, "We're going to surprise a lot of people this year," which has to be true. No matter whether you finish first or last, some folks are bound to be a bit surprised.

Here are some masters of the art in action. "If we stay healthy and show the improvement we're capable of . . . well, I'll take my chances" (Gene Mauch). "We might just surprise everyone. One thing's for sure—it won't be a dull summer." (Don Zimmer). "There's no reason to think we won't be in the middle of things" (Bill Virdon). "We'll be a team to watch" (Pat Corrales). Ralph Houk once quipped, "Who knows what can happen?" This quote may be the finest surviving example of the major-league prediction. It answers one question ("Where will you finish?) with another ("Who knows?") and yet seems deeply satisfying by accepted standards of the craft.

Sometimes even the emptiest prediction can backfire. When Leo Durocher inherited a Cub team that had just finished ninth in a ten-team league, all he could think of to say was

"This is not a ninth-place team." He was right. That year the Cubs finished tenth. Phil Cavaretta, managing another terrible Cub team, once lapsed into candor and said, "We'll be lucky to finish in the first division with this team." One year Chuck Tanner made a dreadful error in predicting that his Pittsburgh Pirates would win the division, the pennant, and the World Series. They did, but that is beside the point. What would baseball be like if everyone went around making accurate, clear predictions? Irony is even worse. Earl Weaver once said of his archrivals, the Yankees, "They have such a great team, I can't see how they can lose any games at all this year."

Tom Lasorda is a ham. When he loses, you get Douglas MacArthur ("We shall return") and when he wins, you get Shakespeare ("Uneasy lies the head that wears a crown"). Joe Torre never got the hang of the preseason prediction. Once he said his terrible Mets team of 1979 would have to be better than the previous year because his young players were a year older, totally overlooking the fact that all the other players in his league were a year older too. Ralph Houk was usually limp. One year he actually said: "I can't say where we'll finish because I don't know what the other clubs will be like," which probably had the same effect on reporters as the pope breaking out into "Heartbreak Hotel" during Mass at the Vatican.

Correctly executed, this annual ritual allows little room for novelty. A good prediction will contain a conditional clause (if everybody stays healthy, if my guys play up to expectations, if we get our share of the breaks, if Bonzo and Goose get out of the Betty Ford clinic, et cetera), followed by a quotable but entirely vaporous declaration (we'll be in the thick of things, nobody can count us out, we can hold our own in this league, anything can happen, et cetera). The manager is allowed to hint, or even say, that his team is a bit better than last year, as long as he makes no claim for the results. Darrell Johnson, while managing the Seattle Mariners, said his team was "potentially" improved, a brilliant bit of hedging that is bound to be widely copied.

A new manager can choose from a list of proven predictions:

- "This year we will be working on fundamentals." (No hope. We can't do anything right.)
- "We have the nucleus of a genuine contender." (About five of our twenty-four guys can play a little.)
- "We can hold our own in this league." (We'll be thrilled to play .500 ball.)
- "This year you'll see the REAL Phillies!" (You're looking at the exact same team that screwed up last year.")
- "This will be a team to watch." (Only if you've already seen everything else on TV and every movie ever made.)
- "This team can beat you a lot of ways." (But none of them come to mind right now.)
- "Youth is the key to this team." (The Joe Torre principle: The future lies ahead.)

When the Yankees were winning every year, downtrodden managers would always observe that "the Yankees put their pants on one leg at a time, just like everybody else." This was meant to convey the idea that the Yankees were not gods (who presumably go around putting on pants both legs at a time), but just pinstriped humans who can surely be beaten by someone, maybe even by a club as bad as mine. Now you no longer hear much about how trousers are put on. The modern version is much more upbeat: "When the big guys look over their shoulders, they're gonna see us coming on!" (As usual, we figure to finish behind the big guys, and all the middle-sized guys, in last place.)

The skipper of a last-place team is always allowed to detect scrappiness in his players, and to predict unspecified excitement. He can call it a "rebuilding" year or tell Vinnie that "We're going to work on fundamentals this season (such as which base to run to if you should ever get a hit). If he runs a team in the American League East, he will be sure to call it "the toughest division in baseball." He can also point out that it's a long season and anything can happen. As Orioles scout Jim Russo once pointed out, "You play a hundred and sixty-two games, and a lot of intangibles come to the surface."

# The
# Luckiest
# Bird-Watcher
# in America

**A**ccording to legend, St. Francis of Assisi had only to spread his arms wide and the birds of the field flew before him and came to rest at his feet. My friend Rudy the bird-watcher gets basically the same effect by simply raising his binoculars. Every time he goes afield, birds line up along his path and pose like muscle-builders. Uncommon birds make a special effort to catch his eye, shrieking or whistling, or perhaps just flapping frantically until he catches on.

When the Kentucky and worm-eating warblers were reported one morning in Central Park, Rudy was determined not to miss them, although he had a super-busy day at his midtown office. At one o'clock, he roared up in a cab, jumped out and ran into the Ramble, saw both birds in five minutes, and still made his lunch date more or less on time. The wonder is that he did not keep the cab waiting.

My explanations do not seem to count much with Rudy. "The Kentucky and worm-eating are hard to find, Rudy," I pointed out patiently. "Nobody sees them in five minutes on the way to lunch." "I only had five minutes," Rudy replied. He pulled off a similar feat in Arizona one summer, seeing both the buff-breasted flycatcher and the violet-crowned hummingbird, during a one-and-a-half-day stopover. These two birds are uncommon to rare, and nobody should rationally expect to see them on a whirlwind stopover. Except Rudy.

The same thing happened when he took a quick trip to the Dry Tortugas in mid-March, hoping to see the white-tailed tropic bird. The bird should never have been there, but apparently it was willing to show up six weeks early so it could make Rudy's life list. In Texas one June, I made the mistake of explaining in advance that Rudy would not get to see a famously rare, furtive, and dull-looking bird not much bigger than its name: the northern beardless tyrannulet. The reason is that by June, it has stopped singing and even its mother probably couldn't find it. But when I left Rudy alone for a minute, the foolhardy tyrannulet popped out of the brush and gave Rudy its full profile for a minute or two while he checked it with his guide. This is the birding equivalent of Greta Garbo coming up to you on the street and asking you out.

Whenever an unusual bird species turns up, we all know it will stay around until Rudy sees it, then leave immediately, perhaps never to be seen again in the hemisphere. In early spring, a greater white-fronted goose, Greenland race, joined a flock of Canada geese near Mecox Bay on Long Island. Rudy was busy and did not show up until the sixteenth day. The goose left that afternoon and was not seen again. In September, I spotted a varied thrush, a bird of the Pacific Coast rain forest, among a flock of robins in my yard in Sag Harbor. Birding cronies descended at once. Rudy could not be found, so the bird naturally hung in there. Eight hours later the ever-confident Rudy ambled in and became, once again, the last known person in the area to see a rare visitor.

Because of this trait, I decided to head up to Concord, Mass., to see the fieldfare reported there in the spring of 1986. No one wants to go all that way and take a chance that the bird may be gone, so I brought Rudy along to make sure it would wait around. We arrived on Sunday, April thirteenth, the fieldfare's eighth day in the area. While we were looking at the bird through our scopes, it fluttered away weakly to the east (apparently exhausted by the long wait for Rudy) and was seen no more.

Rudy's best adventure came on a brief stop in southeast Arizona. He was a neophyte at the time, barely able to tell a Kirtland's warbler from a Holly Farms chicken without important assistance. Since he had a day or two to spare on the way back from a trip to Los Angeles, I suggested he stop off briefly in Tucson and head for the the Santa Rita lodge, only an hour away, to treat himself to some Mexican species, including the elegant trogon, the only relative of the quetzal that nests on U.S. soil.

Rudy called me that night to say things were going badly. "I can't find the trogon," he said, "and I'm stuck out here at a pay phone getting eaten alive by mosquitoes." I asked why he hadn't phoned from the lodge. "The lodge burned down," he said. I told him to stay calm, tomorrow would be brighter, and I gave him directions up Mount Wrightson to the trogon nest.

Tomorrow was indeed brighter. As he headed up the mountain, a stranger said casually, "That's an Aztec thrush over there." Rudy looked, nodded, and wrote it down. Later on the way down, he passed the same spot and came upon a woman who was searching desperately for the bird. "It's over there," quipped Rudy. Nearly unstrung by having the bird of her life pointed out so casually, the woman turned upon Rudy and commenced his birding education at the top of her lungs. "Do you have any idea what that bird is?" she asked in full apoplexy. "It will take you three years to understand what you just saw, three years, do you know that?"

That was just the fifth time that the Aztec thrush had ever been recorded in America. The only surprise to me is that the bird would go to the trouble of showing up four times without Rudy being there. He is now a first-rate birder, and when we go birding together I generally stick close to him, just as many gamblers stay close to their rabbit's foot while visiting Las Vegas. I know that if I head off on my own, the ultimate birding disaster will strike. Rudy will shake his head sadly and explain that I just missed a joint appearance by America's last ivory-billed woodpecker flying along with the last Eskimo curlew.

# Have
# a Martini
# –the Birds
# Will Be
# Right Along

If you are interested in becoming a bird-watcher in the Hamptons, you will need all sorts of good tips, and I can give you one right now: do your very best to avoid the local bird sanctuaries. These refuges give impressive testimony to mankind's fierce love of nature. However, they are usually bird-free. Up at Cedar Point, there is a bird-watcher's trail, which you must avoid, since all the birds do, possibly because they are unable to read the sign. The Morton Wildlife Refuge has a serious national reputation, but I must tell you that I have combed the place for years and never seen an interesting species there. I inform any friends who will listen that they have more chance of seeing vital bird life at Chernobyl.

Once I clambered over a rugged mountain in southeast

Arizona, saw almost nothing, then came back down to the camping-parking lot, full of people eating, screaming, and tossing Frisbees, and there I saw all the birds I was looking for. I sat down wearily on the bank of a stream, and one of the fancy species of the area, the red-faced warbler, flew down to take a bath right in front of me. The reason for this deflating set of affairs is that a great many birds do not like wilderness any more than you do. They prefer nibbling at the edge of human settlements, or it may just seem that way because a lot of wildlife appears where two habitats meet.

This brings me to my backyard in Sag Harbor, the edge of my own little human settlement. The yard is rich in bird life, since it is heavily wooded, has people nearby, and has not yet been declared a bird sanctuary. It also has the understated advantage that you can put your feet up on the deck railing, linger over a martini, and wait for the avian world to come right at you. If you want to be a purist about all this, the martini should be straight up, since most advanced birding is done by ear, and no one wants to lose a great species because of noisy ice cubes.

Early morning is the best time for birding, but I love the late afternoon and early evening. On almost any Friday or Saturday, my fellow birding fanatics Rudy and Billy come over an hour or so before sunset. We break out the Beefeater, scan for birds, and talk about our great good luck at not being in the Morton Wildlife Refuge.

In the wild, birders are supposed to be as quiet as cloistered monks, and we more or less live by that stern rule. But on the deck, with a drink in hand, feet up, we are apt to swap tales of birding triumphs and blunders. In my early days as a birder, when I really did not know what I was doing, I correctly identified a sulphur-bellied flycatcher, fifty feet up, directly overhead, with only a glimpse of a headless underbelly through the canopy. In birding this is the equivalent of a half-court jump-shot that catches only net. On the other hand, I once smartly identified a Clorox bottle as a common egret.

When Billy speaks, he is apt to imply heavily that Rudy and I are obsessives, whereas he leads a balanced birding life, prudently setting some time aside for career and family. The conventional stories about Rudy, as ritualized as the Latin Mass, concern his amazing luck as a birder, and how staggering rarities routinely pop out of the bush on cue whenever he ambles by.

Since birding is not a little old lady's avocation, as everybody tells you, but a macho sport of true blustering swagger, it is absolutely fitting that my deck looks something like a command post. It is nine feet off the ground, perfect for birding, and thirty-three feet wide, which allows a good deal of admiral-like scurrying along the poopdeck when a fast-moving species is spotted. Before we sit down, all unnecessary deck furniture is moved out of the way. No one wants to do the high hurdles if Rudy decides to summon a passenger pigeon or a great auk out of the woods.

In my six years of birding, I have seen more than 250 species on the East End, from Shinnecock to Montauk, and half of them have appeared in or over my backyard. The reason is that the property, though small, has a great variety of habitat: tall trees for warblers and orioles, bare treetops for flycatchers, a lawn for juncos and grackles, a miniforest floor for towhees and ovenbirds, thickets for catbirds and sparrows, a fruit tree for waxwings and other berry-eaters, dead trees for nesting woodpeckers, and a small bog for ducks and wading birds. In the back is a tree with a bare branch where a ruby-throated hummingbird likes to go into torpor, a kind of stupefied rest period. And this year we had new voices at martini time: for the first time, great-crested flycatcher and Carolina wren nested in the yard.

The surprise guest of the spring was mourning warbler, a bird I had looked for all over Texas and then found on Memorial Day in a lilac bush twenty feet from my deck. Even summer, the dullest birding season, provides a good backdrop for happy hour on the deck. Chimney swifts twitter by in their peculiar off-balance flight and maybe a common nighthawk or a scarlet tanager will show up. If there is still some water in the bog, a solitary sandpiper flies in around August tenth, some years with a friend, sometimes solo. A week or so later a northern waterthrush arrives, and in some years, a green-backed heron as well. Two years ago, a yellow-crowned night-heron and a glossy ibis decided to spend Labor Day there, and I set up a telescope so friends could take a look, whether they wanted to or not.

Part of the allure of birding is the mix of predictability and surprise. Frankly, it would ruin my summer if the solitary sandpiper decided to take a year off and not show up in the bog. And the knowledge that new species are always coming through keeps me on my toes. Late last summer I scanned a flock of robins and spotted one with a tell-tale sash across the breast. It was a varied thrush, a bird of the West Coast, and the first sighting from the deck rare enough to be mentioned in *American Birds* magazine. Now, I don't want to become too puffed up about this. I realize that in all probability the thrush was attempting a landing at Morton, overshot its authorized mark, and landed in my tree by mistake. Someday they will doubtlessly have a varied thrush at the refuge. But, alas, so far they haven't. I checked.